MAKING DISCIPLES

The Challenge of Christian Education
at the End of the 20th Century

BY NORMAN E. HARPER

CHRISTIAN STUDIES CENTER

ISBN: 0-939200-04-X

PRINTED IN THE UNITED STATES OF AMERICA

TABLE OF CONTENTS

MAKING DISCIPLES:

The Challenge of Christian Education
at the End of the 20th Century

Norman E. Harper

Dedication

This book is dedicated to the glory of God and to my family—Mary Ida, Maria, Hank, Pepper, Harper, Becky, Jim, and Jay.

Preface

In the absolute sense a disciple is one who self-consciously strives to live the whole of life under the Lordship of Jesus Christ. Defined in this way the making of disciples is the ultimate purpose of all true education.

This points up the need for a book on educational theory and practice that has a rather broad range of readers in view. Thus an attempt has been made to design this book so that it may be used as a textbook or as collateral reading for college or graduate school courses in educational foundations; as resource material for teachers and administrators in Christian schools; as a means of equipping adult leaders in the church and as a source of help and encouragement for concerned parents.

One cannot justify on biblical grounds the idea that a legitimate end can be rightly pursued by illegitimate means. Thus the goal of making disciples requires an educational strategy that is also honoring to God. Such a strategy should include a consideration of the following principles:

1. All education is religious whether it takes place in the church, the home, or the school. Education may be Christian, or it may be based on some other religion, but by its very nature education is religious. While this truth is emphasized throughout the entire work, chapter one has as its special purpose to show the relationship of the Christian faith to the way we think about and practice education in a world that is becoming more and more polarized between those who follow God and those who follow Baal.

2. All educational practice is related to one's view of the educand—the person to be educated. In this connection chapter two sets forth some of the most important educational implications of a biblical view of the nature of man.

3. The family, the school, and the church have distinctive but complementary roles in the task of making disciples. Chapters three, four, and five show how this responsibility may be carried out in each of these primary educational agencies on the basis of a Christian world and life view.

4. The most important factor to the child, humanly speaking, in the teaching-learning process is the teacher. Chapter six examines the role of the Christian teacher from a Christian theistic perspective.

5. The humanistic theories of education in the world today which compete for our allegiance make it imperative for the Christian educator to understand these theories and be able to

evaluate them critically. Chapter seven provides at least a beginning for coming to terms with three of the most influential contemporary non-Christian views of education.

This book grew out of a series of lectures on Christian education given in June, 1973, under the sponsorship of Christian Studies Center. At that time Mr. R. M. Metcalf and Mr. Don Kimsey, the founder and executive director respectively of Christian Studies Center, asked me to prepare these lectures for publication. A considerable amount of time elapsed, however, before I was able to comply with their request. During the interim some of the lecture material was used in revised form at the Pensacola Theological Institute in August, 1974: at a regional meeting of the Evangelical Theological Society in December, 1975; and at the Belhaven College World and Life Conference in May, 1980. The original lectures have been revised substantially for publication.

All quotations from the Scripture in this book are from the American Standard Version unless otherwise specified.

So many people are to be thanked for their contribution to the preparation of this manuscript that it is hard to know where to begin. Perhaps the best place to start is with Mrs. Barbara Burgess who not only did a significant amount of the typing, but also provided editorial assistance. Others who helped with the typing are: Mrs. Becky Chaplin, Mrs. Fonda Davies, Miss Sally Gaskin, Mrs. Mary Jane Herwick, Miss Sandra Lewis and Mrs. Tammie Matlack. For editorial help and gentle prodding to complete the manuscript, I would like to express my appreciation to Mr. Douglas Petersen, the present executive director of Christian Studies Center.

I am very indebted to my colleague, Dr. John R. deWitt, who read the entire manuscript except for chapter six and made a number of helpful suggestions. Sincere appreciaton is also expressed to other colleagues who have either suggested references or interacted with me concerning some part of the book. They are: Dr. Knox Chamblin, Professor A. H. Freundt, Dr. Simon Kistemaker, Dr. Paul Kooistra, Dr. William Stanway and Professor Richard Watson.

For their patience and understanding in allowing me to try out some of the ideas discussed in this book, my heartfelt thanks goes to the First Presbyterian Church of Clarksdale, Mississippi, and to the Presbyterian Day School of the same city. A sincere word of appreciation is also due to the Board of Trustees and administration of Reformed Theological Seminary for their support. For her prayers, encouragement, and serving as my sounding board, warm thanks go to my wife. And last, but by no means least, I would like to express my gratitude to all my students who through the years have helped make teaching for me a labor of love.

1

A POINT OF VIEW

"For of Him, and through Him, and unto Him, are all things. To Him be the glory forever. Amen." (Romans 11:36)

No one thinks it strange that there are over 250 religious bodies in the United States today. "After all," it is said, "religion is highly subjective. Its substance cannot be confirmed in the marketplace by some objectively verifiable public test. Everyone, therefore, has the right to his own opinion. One view is as good as another."

At the same time, it is accepted that subjects such as science, mathematics, or even psychology and education involve objective facts that are not subject to interpretation. When people differ in these areas, it is only because they do not have all the facts.

The idea that certain areas of reality can be known without interpretation, and viewed from a neutral point of view must be challenged. Every human being has faith in something which affects his understanding of everything. Church and state or church and school may be separated, but religion cannot be separated from any area of human activity or thought. The premise that facts may be objectively known, absolutely uninfluenced by the faith of the knower, is simply untrue.

Can you imagine a non-Christian behavioristic psychologist objectively describing a Christian's conversion experience or a child's temper tantrum absolutely uninfluenced by his belief

1

that man is an empty organism, totally conditioned by his environment? Is it conceivable that a non-Christian pragmatic educator would exercise discipline in a classroom without any regard to his view that there are no absolute moral values? Both men's beliefs are grounded, not on self-evident facts, but on a commitment to a non-demonstrable faith principle.

God is the author of all truth; therefore, the truth of science agrees with the truth of Christianity. The Christian is motivated to search out every aspect of the universe, knowing that when all the facts are revealed, the result can only confirm his faith. When the non-Christian interprets some aspect of reality from a man-centered point of view, the conflict is not between faith and fact, as we are sometimes led to believe. Rather, it is a conflict between Christian faith and non-Christian faith. The Christian and the non-Christian bring to any given data an interpretation that rests upon irreconcilable faith principles.

The German word *weltanschauung* is the term used to indicate a world view or world perspective. Man cannot know everything, but he can and does consider everything as a whole from the standpoint of a particular philosophy or theology, whether or not he is able to articulate it.

The idea of a world view or perspective is not new. It is rooted deeply in human nature. Man is a rational being and he is inwardly compelled to make sense out of his world. This is true even for those who have concluded that life is absolutely absurd. The very conclusion that nothing makes sense is a way of getting a handle on the nature of reality. As James Orr has said: "It [the mind] is not content with fragmentary knowledge, but tends constantly to rise from facts to laws, from laws to higher laws, from these to the highest generalizations possible."[1]

[1]James Orr, *The Christian View of God and the World* (Grand Rapids: Wm. B. Eerdmans Publishing Company, 1954), p. 6.

A Christian *weltanschauung* is a comprehensive, unified, and all-pervasive system of thought. It offers an explanation of the origin, purpose, and nature of everything.

Loving God with all his heart, mind, and soul, the Christian has a distinctive outlook on the world. In whatever measure he is faithful to his Lord, he self-consciously begins with the sovereign triune God in every area of his thought. In this connection, Abraham Kuyper, describing what he believed to be the only consistent Christian world-and-life view, stated:

> God is present in all life, with the influence of His omnipresent and almighty power, and no sphere of human life is conceivable in which religion does not maintain its demands that God shall be praised, that God's ordinances shall be observed, and that every *labora* shall be permeated with its *ora* in fervent and ceaseless prayer. Wherever man may stand, whatever he may do, to whatever he may apply his hand, in agriculture, in commerce, and in industry, or his mind, in the world of art, and science, he is, in whatsover it may be, constantly standing before the face of his God, he is employed in the service of his God, he has strictly to obey his God, and above all, he has to aim at the glory of his God.[2]

God is absolutely sovereign. The expression of His mind and will in the Scripture is, therefore, completely authoritative for faith and practice. God has given to man in the Holy Scriptures a transcendent norm by which all of life is to be rightly understood and governed. As Henry J. Stob declared:

[2]Abraham Kuyper, *Christianity as a Life-System: The Witness of a World-View* (Memphis: Christian Studies Center, 1981), p. 17.

Christian philosophy posits the inadequacy of a merely immanentistic approach to an understanding of the cosmos, and assumes the necessity of a transcendent vantage point. This means that it deliberately proposes to interpret the created world in the light of the Christian Scriptures. In doing so it denies that it is sacrificing its claim to the name philosophy. The Christian philosopher repudiates the dogmatism that would make the human consciousness autonomous and philosophy a purely intellectual enterprise. He insists, on the contrary, that the beginning of an adequate interpretation of the world can be made only when a thinker allows himself to be instructed by that world's maker and interpreter, only when a philosopher enrolls himself in the school of God.[3]

The Christian, informed by the Word of God, knows that everythings comes from God, is sustained by Him, and is directed to His glory (Rom. 11:36). He is persuaded that in Christ "all things hold together" (Col. 1:17). He is committed to living the whole of life by the grace of God under the Lordship of Christ.

In contrast, a non-Christian's *weltanschauung* is directed by his reason, his experience, or his existential choice. He seeks to explain the origin, purpose, and nature of reality on the basis of himself as the final arbiter of truth.

In the twentieth century, man, disillusioned with the fruits of an earthbound rationalism, has turned to an even more sub-

---

[3]Henry J. Stob, "The Word of God and Philosophy," in *The Word of God and the Reformed Faith* (Grand Rapids: Baker Book House, 1943), p. 111.

jective view of life. Francis Schaeffer has aptly pointed out that modern man, carrying out the logical implications of Kierkegaardianism, is trying to "understand the world by starting totally from himself, even though it has led him to give up hope for a unified field of knowledge and confidence in rationality. . . ."[4] Today one has only to thoughtfully consider the most popular art forms to see the pervasive influence of man's irrationalism in the world. Whether the artist uses paint, sound, or written word, the message is the same: "There is no truth, no meaning, no moral absolute".

Many years ago when I was a boy I heard a speaker tell the following story: "A certain factory worker had the responsibility of blowing the whistle every day at precisely 12:00 noon. In order to be sure of the correct time, he set his own watch by a clock on the wall of a local jewelry store. After doing this for some time, it occurred to him that the jewelry store owner had to have some standard by which he could set his clock. Thus, one day when he was in the store, he inquired of the owner, 'Sir, how do you know what time to set your clock?' The jewelry store owner replied, 'Well, you see, on the other side of town there is a factory and every day precisely at noon they blow a whistle. . . .'"

The point of the story is obvious. Modern man takes counsel only from himself or from others in the same predicament. When the contemporary educator acknowledges no transcendent norm, he really has no basis for saying that one educational theory or practice is right and another is wrong.

God or man, that is the question. The Christian educator should not vacillate between two opinions.

Christian philosophy views the world in its entirety from the vantage point of Scripture. A Christian philosophy of educa-

[4]Francis Schaeffer, "The Irrationality of Modern Thought," *Christianity Today,* XV, No. 5 (December 4, 1970), pp. 10-11.

tion is a comprehensive approach to all aspects of the teaching-learning process, including the agencies of education, according to the principles set forth in the Word of God. Thus, one should not think of himself as a Christian and as an educator, as though one's faith and vocation are unrelated. The Christian educator must fulfill the whole of his task so that all that is involved in being an educator is shaped by all that is implied in the name Christian.

It will be the purpose of the following chapters to explore, at least in a preliminary way, some of the basic educational implications of a God-centered world and life view and then to distinguish a Christian view of education from several current non-Christian theories.

2

THE NATURE OF MAN
AND CHRISTIAN EDUCATION

*"And God created man in His own image, in
the image of God created He him; male and
female created He them."* (Gen. 1:27)

What one believes about the nature of man lies right at the
heart of the educative process. Bavinck[1] stated accurately that
"all great pedagogical movements proceed consciously or un-
consciously, implicitly or explicitly from a general conception
of the nature of man."[2]
Non-Christian views of man generally regard him as the
product of evolutionary selection and environmental conditioning. The pragmatist assumes that man is a behaving organism with the capacity to expand his present experience. The behaviorist believes that man is a machine and can be programmed to operate according to the desires of the program-
mer, who has already been programmed to program others.
The existentialist postulates that man is an autonomous individual who is the architect of his own life.

---

[1]Herman Bavinck, the great 19th century Dutch theologian, saw the implications of
Reformed thought for education and made a significant contribution in his works on
educational philosophy and psychology, c.f. *Principles of Education; The New Education;* and *Principles of Psychology.*

[2]Cornelius Jaarsma, *The Educational Philosophy of Herman Bavinck* (Grand
Rapids: Wm. B. Eerdmans Publishing Company, 1935), p. 137.

These humanistic views of man and their corresponding approaches to education will be considered in chapter seven. In this chapter we will explore the educational implications of the biblical doctrine of man.

THE BIBLICAL DOCTRINE OF MAN

Genesis 1:27 says: "And God created man in His own image, in the image of God created He him; male and female created He them." That human beings were made like God is a sobering and sublime truth. To say that man is God is blasphemy; however, to say that man is like God is to identify him truly and assign to him his rightful place as the crown of creation. A Christian friend involved in small group work remarked to me, "Everyone in the group seems to be preoccupied with the question, Who am I? I don't know whether there is something wrong with me or not, but I think I know who I am." She was right. She did know who she was. As a Christian, she knew she was a person made in the image of God.

The question then arises, Of what does the image of God consist? In what way is man like God? Does this image refer to some particular characteristic of man, such as his reason or his capacity to know right and wrong? Certainly it includes these qualities. But the Scripture implies by its language that whatever is essential to being "man" was created "in the image of God."

The Genesis passage also teaches that there is no distinction of worth between male and female, for both were made in the image of God. Moreover, the Apostle Paul declares that in Christ "there can be no male and female" (Gal. 3:28), indicating that in the family of God such distinctions are transcended in a higher unity. There are, however, other passages (Gen. 2:18 ff., Eph. 5:22ff.) that make it equally clear that there is a distinction of function intended in creation in which male and female complement each other to their mutual fulfillment and honor.

Human life is precious in the sight of God, as is further brought out in Genesis 9:6: "Whoso sheddeth man's blood, by man shall his blood be shed: for in the image of God made He man." Man's life is of such great value that capital punishment is demanded as the only appropriate penalty for one who willfully and maliciously takes the life of another human being. The laws of various states providing for capital punishment for premeditated murder are a continual reminder that human life is priceless.

The special glory and distinctive characteristic of man is that he is made in the image of God. Man has in common with all created things the fact that he is created. But though he has many functions and traits in common with animals, man alone is made like God and is entrusted with the responsibility of exercising dominion over the rest of creation. As the psalmist wrote:

> For Thou hast made him but little lower than
>   God,
> And crownest him with glory and honor.
> Thou makest him to have dominion over the
>   works of thy hands;
> Thou hast put all things under his feet:
> All sheep and oxen,
> Yea, and the beasts of the field,
> The birds of the heavens, and the fish of the
>   sea,
> Whatsoever passeth through the paths of the
>   seas
> (Ps. 8:5–8).

Man had a glorious beginning, but the story doesn't end

here. In the Genesis account we read:

> And Jehovah God took the man, and put him into the garden of Eden to dress it and to keep it. And Jehovah God commanded the man, saying, Of every tree of the garden thou mayest freely eat: but of the tree of the knowledge of good and evil, thou shalt not eat of it: for in the day that thou eatest thereof thou shalt surely die (Gen. 2:15-17).

Genesis 3 reveals that our first parents disobeyed God by eating of the forbidden fruit. The Apostle Paul, writing about the effect of the sin of Adam, said: "Therefore, as through one man sin entered into the world, and death through sin; and so death passed unto all men, for that all sinned" (Rom. 5:12). According to the Westminster Shorter Catechism this passage is understood to mean: "The covenant being made with Adam, not only for himself, but for his posterity, all mankind, descending from him by ordinary generation, sinned in him, and fell with him, in his first transgression."[3] It is further understood that "the fall brought mankind into an estate of sin and misery."[4]

Before the fall man had a true interpretation of reality, his will was conformed to the divine will, and he desired nothing other than to do that which was pleasing to his heavenly Father. As a result of the fall, man stands under the curse of the Adamic sin. Every part of his being is affected by sin. His will is perverted, his intellect enfeebled, his emotions debased. We are "by nature children of wrath" (Eph. 2:3).

[3]The Westminster Shorter Catechism, Q. 16.
[4]*Ibid.*, answer to Q. 17.

10

Although the image is corrupted and deformed, man is still the image of God and the object of God's sovereign grace. The whole man was made in the image of God. The whole man was affected by the fall. Thanks be to God that through the life, death, and resurrection of Jesus Christ and the renewing grace of the Holy Spirit, the whole man may be redeemed.

A biblical view of the nature of man suggests a number of implications for Christian education.

IDENTIFICATION

Self-identification. When the student begins to struggle with the question of who he is—as he almost inevitably does—the Christian teacher has an answer. He doesn't have to abandon the student to an endless and futile quest for a reply to an unanswerable question. The teacher can say to the student, "You are made like God. There is something very unique and special about your life and the life of your neighbor, who is also made in the image of God."

The answer is brought home to the student as he is nurtured in an atmosphere of mutual respect and dignity appropriate even for broken images of God. Any sense of being manipulated as a machine or conditioned as an animal gives the student a very distorted view of himself. It is essential, therefore, that he be taught as a person in the context of a personal relationship.

The teacher must help the student see himself and others not only in terms of the original creation but also with respect to the sin and misery resulting from the fall, and then with regard to the immeasurable benefits of the redemptive work of Jesus Christ. When the student sees himself as a sinner saved by grace; when he applies, even in some elementary way, the implications of his faith to his task as a student; and when he is moved to reach out to others and share with them from his own life the truth and love of Christ, then he has a real awareness of

11

who he is and who his neighbor is.

What has been said about the student, of course, can also be said about the teacher. As a human being he has the same origin, the same need, and the same hope. The teacher as well as the student must be teachable.

Distinction between the roles of the teacher and student. Teacher and student, although both made in the image of God and by nature sinners, do not have the same function in the teaching-learning process, as some contemporary educators seem to assert. For example, William Ramsay, writing on the role of the teacher, tells with apparent approval the procedure followed in a class he visited. He wrote: "After one man led an opening prayer, a woman briefly reviewed the previous week's discussion. Then a married couple presided over the study, alternately asking and commenting on questions related to the study book. Much of the conversation centered around a report prepared by a third man. By the end of the hour nearly every member of that group had shared in the considerations."[5] Commenting further on the class, he observed, "Had I not been introduced to the leading couple before entering the room, I would never have been quite certain who were teachers and who were students. They all seemed to be studying together."[6]

The use of the discussion method, of course, is not the point at issue. This method, along with any other method, may be consistently used by the Christian theist as long as the method is not an end in itself, but is a means to the end of knowing the truth. The above illustration was cited only to show the trend toward eliminating the distinction of role between teacher and

[5]William Ramsay, "The Changing Role of the Teacher," *Dimensions in Christian Education*, XVI, No. 6 (November-December, 1966), p. 29.
[6]*Ibid.*

student. In the 50s and 60s it was fashionable to call the teacher of the class the "leader of the group." Now it is said that the most effective group leader is one who can become so much a part of the group that he cannot be identified as the leader. This trend tends to parallel the simultaneous trend away from the teaching of objective truth toward the sharing of experiences, and subsequently from the sharing of experiences to the group's doing its own thing without structure or purpose.

Teaching the truth and love of God is best done when the teacher and student know who they are and what their respective roles are in the teaching-learning process.

Distinction between the role of male and female in the school curriculum. There is a trend today to label all distinctions between male and female as sexism, an "ism" which, it is thought, must be avoided at all costs. Elementary reading books which reflect stereotyped roles for boys and girls or courses of study limited to one sex, such as domestic arts or athletic activities, are examples of the school programs in question. In some quarters even a style of dress readily identified with one sex is suspect.

It must be admitted that a distinction of function between male and female has often led to a distinction of worth. In 1972 the National Organization for Women in Princeton, New Jersey, published the result of a two-year study of reading series used in elementary schools. In the course of the study almost 3,000 stories were analyzed. In these stories, the researchers found the ratio of boys to girls to be 5 to 2. The ratio of stories with an adult male character to those with an adult female was 3 to 1. The ratio of male biographies to female biographies was 6 to 1. Clever girls appeared 33 times, clever boys 131 times. This kind of inequity is, of course, indefensible.[7]

[7]Olive Gogdill, "Now It's Goodbye to Dick and Jane Stories," *The Clarion Ledger-Jackson Daily News*, Sunday, July 14, 1974, Section G. p. 1.

What is the solution to these and similar inequities? Should we eliminate the distinction between the role of male and female as proposed by the National Organization for Women? Should we develop a unisex approach to personal relationships as some social anarchists advocate? Each of these proposals can be attacked on various theoretical and practical grounds, but the primary reason for rejecting them is that they are clearly out of harmony with the law of God.

The Word of God makes it very clear that in the family, the most basic unit of human society, the man and woman are to assume different roles (Eph. 5:21–6:4). The husband is to be the head of the wife. The wife is to be submissive to her husband.

The headship of the husband over the wife is patterned after the headship of Christ over the church. This beautiful Scriptural design envisions a rule of love in a family government the purpose of which is to facilitate the realization of each person's fullest potential and to bring the greatest honor and glory to the heavenly Father.

God created woman as a helper suitable for man. She is of the same nature and rank, yet uniquely equipped mentally, physically, and emotionally to complete the one for whom she was made. As a helpmeet, the wife is the alter ego of her husband, serving as his spiritual, emotional, and sexual partner. The Christian wife does not compete with her husband. She acts instead as his companion and inspirer.

The woman quite naturally finds the idea of submission hard to accept. It seems so demeaning for one human being to be submissive to another. If, however, one person submits to another because God commands it, then ultimately the submission is not to man, but to God.

The Lord Jesus Christ Himself is the supreme example of man submitting to man in order to accomplish the Father's will. It is beyond the grasp of human understanding that the

Lord of all would condescend to become the servant of all. Nevertheless, Christ Jesus,

> . . . existing in the form of God, counted not the being on an equality with God a thing to be grasped, but emptied Himself, taking the form of a servant, being made in the likeness of men; and being found in fashion as a man, He humbled Himself, becoming obedient even unto death, yea, the death of the cross (Phil. 2:6–8).

There is something very Christ-like about the Christian woman who submits herself to her own husband as unto the Lord out of a genuine desire to do the will of God. Such a woman of God may confidently expect her loving obedience to result in the ennobling of her life and the best possible use of the gifts with which she has been endowed.

A distinction of function, therefore, does not necessarily imply a distinction of worth. It is only as the biblical distinction of function between male and female is maintained that either can realize his or her true worth, which is both equal and complementary. When male and female fulfill their divinely ordained roles, God is honored and the social order is blessed. The school program, including the courses of study, the content and illustrations in textbooks, and the athletic activities must provide for a biblical diversity that enables all students to complement one another in their common task as servants of Christ.

TEACHING-LEARNING PROCESS

Man consists of both body and soul. The whole person—body and soul—is made in the image of God and is the crown of God's handiwork. It is the whole person that was corrupted

15

by the fall of Adam, is redeemed through Jesus Christ, is restored into the perfect image of God, and inhabits eternity.

The teaching-learning process, therefore, focuses upon the whole person. One dimension of the student, such as his intellect, cannot be developed without regard to his emotions, physiological functions, and social relationships. We must continually be concerned with the whole child in his present life situation.

However, it may aid our understanding of the functions of the whole person to single out and consider the educational implications of some of those qualities that are peculiar to man as the image of God.

Immeasurable potential. As the image of God, man is positioned above nature and has a potential which cannot be fully measured by human analysis. We can determine a student's height and weight, but we cannot with the same degree of accuracy ascertain his capacity to know, to understand, to appreciate, or to achieve. In this connection entirely too much confidence is placed in our testing procedures designed to examine every facet of the student's personality.

A student makes "C's" on school exams, scores 100 on an I.Q. test (middle average), and takes a vocational preference test which shows he will probably do best in an outdoor occupation in which he has little leadership responsibility. Is this all that can be said? Do we now have a complete profile of the student? If not, is it simply a matter of devising a better instrument? If we accept a biblical view of man, the answer is no.

In a note to parents on a report card which I helped to design are found these words of caution: "The purpose of this report is to help you as a parent to evaluate your child's progress academically, personally, and socially insofar as we are able to measure this." Here is an attempt to keep before the parent the limitations of testing and grading. Both parent and teacher are reminded that there is never an adequate rationale for consigning a student to a particular category beyond which he cannot go.

A former student of mine took a standard I.Q. test on which he scored 99 (a low average). Not taking the test too seriously and being a very conscientious student, he went on to graduate in the top 25% of his class. His friends sometimes referred to him as "99." They weren't making fun of the student; they were showing their disdain for the test.

The worrisome little boy in the back row of the classroom who is usually misbehaving and rarely pays attention cannot be dismissed by the teacher as one who will never amount to anything. He may grow up to be the teacher's principal or perhaps, even more ironically, his pastor.

The point here is not to eliminate testing and grading, but to keep all types of student evaluation in perspective. Dealing with the student as though he differs from an animal only by being a more complex organism is both unbiblical and unscientific.

Although the student should be encouraged to be realistic about his gifts, he should be challenged to pursue his studies in the full assurance that he can do whatever God wants him to do, through Jesus Christ who strengthens him (Phil. 4:13).

Rationality. One of the qualities that most distinguishes man as the image of God from animal life is his ability to reason and to act on the basis of his reason. Bavinck puts it this way:

> Animals, at least the higher animals, do have the same sense organs as man, and can sense things (hear, see, smell, taste, and feel). They can form images or pictures, and relate these images to each other. But animals do not have reason, cannot separate the image from the particular, individual and concrete thing. They

17

cannot . . .raise [images] into concepts, cannot
relate the concepts and so form judgments,
cannot make inferences from the judgments
nor arrive at decisons, and cannot carry out the
decisions by an act of the will.[8]

The transmission of knowledge from one person to another
or from one generation to another presupposes that God has
rationally structured the world and that man can understand
the world that God has made. That man has the capacity to
reason, and that his reason is like the reason of the Creator
who designed the universe, is the only explanation for the
development of language and science, and in fact, for the
whole of human culture.

Unfortunately, the rational character of the student is not
always taken into consideration in the modern school. Too
often the emphasis is on rote learning rather than understanding. Sometimes the student is so conditioned to just memorizing facts that only with great difficulty can he adjust to an
academic environment which requires him to think. In this
regard a former professional teacher, an unusually gifted and
perceptive young lady, related this experience to me:

> I found in making out tests for my ninth
> graders that students could answer fill-in-the-
> blank or completion questions which were
> worded in exactly the same way that the
> material was worded in their textbooks or
> notes which I had given them. But if I changed
> simply the order of the words, some of the

[8]Herman Bavinck, *Our Reasonable Faith* (Grand Rapids: Wm. B. Eerdmans Publishing Company, 1956), p. 200.

same students were unable to give a correct answer. Apparently they could fit the word in a certain order, but they had no real grasp of the whole idea which was supposedly being learned.

Even on study questions, where students were reading material and searching for answers in their textbooks, they were often unable to find the answer when the question was worded differently from the sentences they were reading.

Only a small minority were able to pull together and sort material they had studied in such a way that they could answer an overview type question, much less answer one requiring them to draw deductions or conclusions from what they had read.

Every experienced teacher who has attempted to help students see relationships and make judgments can recall numerous similar experiences that were equally frustrating. Of even greater concern to the thoughtful Christian teacher, however, is when the student conditioned to rote learning has the same problem transferring this kind of training to life situations.

It is not my intent to discourage all memorization, especially not of the Scriptures. The words of the psalmist, "Thy word have I laid up in my heart, that I might not sin against thee" (Ps. 119:11), are often quoted in support of memorizing Bible verses. But let the Scriptures be taught for understanding before they are memorized, in keeping with the psalmist's prayer: "Give me understanding, and I shall keep thy law; yea, I shall observe it with my whole heart" (Ps. 119:34).

For a person to understand a concept, he must be able to interpret it in the light of his presuppositions, relate it to previously known concepts, and apply it in appropriate situations. Teaching with this goal in mind naturally follows from a biblical view of the student's capacity to reason. What a change this practice would bring to modern education!

Responsibility. As a religious being, man is responsible to God for every act, thought, and deed. The capacity of man to respond self-consciously to God's claim on the whole of his life is an essential element of what it means to be human.

James Orr wrote: "As a free, spiritual, self-determining cause, standing at the summit of nature, man is . . . in a very marked sense the image of his Maker. It is this power of will and self-decision in man which most of all constitutes him as a person."[9] Isn't this the implication of such passages as: "I call heaven and earth to record this day against you, that I have set before you life and death, blessing and cursing: therefore choose life, that both thou and thy seed may live" (Deut. 30:19, KJV). Consider also: "And the Spirit and the bride say, Come. And let him that heareth say, Come. And let him that is athirst come. And whosoever will, let him take the water of life freely" (Rev. 22:17, KJV). If this is true, then man can act in ways unexplainable by environmental causes. He is more than a machine, more than an animal. He may justly be praised when he has done well and blamed when he has done wrong.

There are, it must be observed, limits to man's freedom. Even in a state of innocence he did not have the absolute power of contrary choice, that is, the freedom to choose uninfluenced by his own nature. Since the Fall, man has not had the power to do that which is good apart from the renewing grace of the Holy Spirit. In this regard, Calvin said that man is ". . . not deprived of will, but of soundness of will. . . . Therefore simply

[9]James Orr, *The Christian View of God and the World* (Grand Rapids: Wm. B. Eerdmans Publishing Company, 1954), p. 140.

to will is of man; to will ill, of a corrupt nature; to will well, of grace."[10]

If man is indeed a responsible being, how can this be applied in the classroom? First of all, both teacher and student must recognize that they are accountable to God for the way they participate in the teaching-learning process.

The teacher who takes seriously the claims of Christ will prepare for his classes and perform his task as one who is answerable to God. When his students do poor work, his first thought will be to examine his own methods. He will ask himself questions such as: Have I made the purpose of the course clear? Have I adapted my teaching methods and means of evaluation to the objectives of the course? Have I been unrealistic in my expectations of the students?

The student, of course, is also accountable for whether or not he learns, a fact that many contemporary educators are not willing to admit. "If the student doesn't learn," it is said, "the teacher hasn't taught." That may or may not be true in a given situation. It is certainly not axiomatic. As a responsible being, the student must give an account of his stewardship in carrying out his academic tasks. He must choose to study. It is not something he will do automatically if properly motivated by the teacher.

The following case seems fairly typical. The time has come for Tom to do his homework. There is no reasonable excuse for delay. On the desk before him are his books, paper and pencil, together with instructions for doing the assignment. He has at least some understanding of the value of the assignment in terms of achieving worthwhile goals. But what does he do? He adjusts his chair, sharpens his pencil, gets a Coke, looks at

---

[10]John Calvin, *Institutes of the Christian Religion,* translated by Henry Beveridge, Vol. I (Grand Rapids: Wm. B. Eerdmans Publishing Company, 1962), p. 253.

another television program—in short, he does anything to postpone the time of opening his book and bringing his mind to bear upon the printed page. Why? Because a person's using his mind to concentrate, to think, to evaluate, and to draw conclusions is a costly process. Study requires intellectual effort. There is no way to eliminate the necessity for this self-conscious mental activity, even for the most highly motivated student.

There is also a volitional element in the way the learner relates to the truth to be learned. That is, the student not only has to choose to concentrate on the printed page, pay attention to what is being said, or thoughtfully participate in a class discussion, but, in addition, having understood the truth being presented, he must commit himself to it. Dr. Cornelius Jaarsma put it this way:

> As religious being the subject accepts or rejects as truth or error what is disclosed to him in conceptualizing. In understanding he generalizes and forms concepts. Concepts unfold to him as rational-moral-social-esthetic-free-responsible being an area of truth to which he is given to commit himself. A person is not merely a growing organism in whom developmental patterns of behavior begin to take form. He is a religious being whose very nature is to ferret out truth for commitment.[11]

Commitment, then, as well as understanding, is involved in all learning. Suppose we want to teach the child the Bible verse:

[11]Cornelius Jaarsma, *Human Development, Learning and Teaching* (Grand Rapids: Wm. B. Eerdmans Publishing Company, 1959), p. 281.

"Believe on the Lord Jesus, and thou shalt be saved" (Acts 16:31). The child memorizes the words without understanding their meaning and without commitment to the truth revealed in the text. Yet there is both understanding and commitment. When the child is asked the question, "What must one do to be saved?" he understands and is committed to the activity of repeating the words, "Believe on the Lord Jesus, and thou shalt be saved." However, if we really want to reach the child with the Gospel, we will have to take time to be sure that he understands who Jesus is and what it means to believe on Him.

There are no teaching methods, however, that will guarantee commitment. The teacher can encourage and exhort the child to respond, but the individual himself, as he is enabled by the Holy Spirit, makes the choice to accept the truth in his heart. Moreover, this inward commitment is prior to authentic outward behavior.

This principle is illustrated by Jesus in the parable of the sower: "And that in the good ground, these are such as in an honest and good heart, having heard the word, hold it fast, and bring forth fruit with patience" (Luke 8:15).

The capacity for "nondeficit motivation." [12] The secular educational psychologist, with his naturalistic view of man, carries on his work in the area of learning theory on the assumption that the primary stimulus for learning is one's desire to satisfy personal needs such as hunger, thirst, pain, fatigue, fear, anxiety, and insecurity. When there is tension within the individual as a result of some physical or emotional need, he is inwardly aroused to move toward equilibrium. For example, a student is stimulated to study carefully and re-

---

[12]Although dealt with here in a different way, the author is indebted to Robert R. Boehlke, *Theories of Learning in Christian Education* (Philadelphia: The Westminster Press, 1962), pp. 53–56.

hearse a speech which he is to give before the class in order to satisfy a felt need for recognition. In receiving the acclaim of his peers and the praise of his teacher, he is inwardly relieved of tension as his urge for self-acceptance is fulfilled. This is "deficit motivation."

That human learning ordinarily has its inception in felt needs and that the teacher should relate the material to be learned to those needs is not in question. The issue is whether or not there is in man a basis for motivation that goes beyond the satisfaction of personal needs and, if so, what difference this makes in the way the Christian teacher should motivate the student.

From a biblical point of view, man has the capacity to transcend self-interest. Jesus said to His disciples, "if any man would come after me, let him deny himself, and take up his cross, and follow me. For whosoever would save his life shall lose it: and whosoever shall lose his life for my sake shall find it" (Matt. 16:24,25). His appeal was based on their commitment to One greater than self. As disciples of Christ they were called to do His will even at the cost of suffering need. Every task, therefore, including the tasks involved in the learning process, may be self-consciously performed in terms of one's commitment to Jesus Christ. In this event, all other motives are subordinate to and consistent with the primary motive.

"But," someone objects, "not everyone who comes to your class is a Christian and is able to be motivated to learn out of a commitment to Christ. Moreover, believers and non-believers have legitimate needs and interests that should be explored as ways of motivating them toward sound academic performances." This is true. If, however, Christ alone is worthy of our total and unconditional commitment, then no personal need or interest should be given that place in a person's life. To do so is nothing short of idolatry, reinforcing the self-centeredness into which we are born as descendants of Adam.

How then can the teacher present Christ as the One before whom all other things must be subordinate, and at the same time not ignore the divinely ordained needs of the student? The answer is discussed here only in a brief and summary way. First of all, throughout the year the teacher should make it clear by precept and example that the primary impetus for any activity is the knowledge that such activity would exalt Christ and accomplish His purpose. Only the believer, of course, who has a conscious awareness of his identity as a disciple of Christ, is moved to act in this way. But the non-believer as well as the believer needs to have this appeal set before him.

Secondly, the teacher should keep in a biblical perspective what has already been referred to as subordinate motives. Paul does this when he instructs the congregation at Thessalonica: "if any will not work, neither let him eat" (2 Thess. 3:10). The incentive is stated clearly and simply. It is not overdone. Undoubtedly if Paul's command were enforced, the average person, whether believer or non-believer, would be highly motivated to do an honest day's work. But Paul does not imply in any way that the meeting of one's physical needs is the chief end of life.

The satisfaction of emotional needs is also a very powerful stimulus to all kinds of human behavior. With the current man-centered emphasis pervading the media and varied educational agencies, it is understandable that many people are so preoccupied with their own needs that they find it difficult, if not impossible, to look beyond their own lives to the needs of others. Modern man seems to be saying, "the most important thing in all of life to me is my own personal happiness." This, of course, is not only woefully wrong, it is also ultimately unsatisfying. And this attitude is the inevitable result of treating as ultimate in importance that which is by its nature subordinate.

A church school official asks, "Should we give an award to

25

children for memorizing Bible verses or the Catechism?'' It all depends on how it is done. If the real emphasis is placed on the value and importance of what is learned and if not too much is made of the award, then the giving of an award for academic achievement can help the child gain greater self-respect without pandering to his ego. The same may be said about the use of praise as a means of motivation. The teacher ought freely and sincerely to praise the child when he has done well, but he should never praise the child indiscriminately or lavishly.

When ''deficit motivation'' is treated by the teacher as subordinate to and consistent with ''nondeficit motivation''— the inward prompting to act out of love for Christ—then the needs of the person, believer or non-believer, are most effectively met and God is truly honored.

But aren't man's deepest and most fundamental needs spiritual? Is it possible to overly stress a person's need for Christ? Certainly we cannot overemphasize the sufficiency of God to meet human need. He is indeed the great *El Shaddai,* the source of all comfort and blessing. Neither can we say too much about the invitation of God's Word to ''draw near with boldness unto the throne of grace, that we may receive mercy, and may find grace to help in time of need'' (Heb. 4:16).

A problem occurs, however, when we present Christ almost exclusively as the One who satisfies all our needs, and rarely ever present Him as the Lord of glory who has an absolute claim upon our lives. This danger can be illustrated by those groups that approach the study of the Scriptures from an anthropocentric point of view, that is, concentrating on questions such as, What does the passage mean to *me* and how does it meet *my* needs? Often this type of approach omits questions such as, What does the passage tell me about *God* and the duties *He* requires of me? Of course, we need to know the answers to all these questions, but a proper understanding derives only from a theocentric perspective, which man can hold and is indeed responsible to maintain.

The capacity for fellowship. Along with the worth and value of the individual personality, the factor which has chiefly occupied our attention thus far, there is the sociality of man. God made man a social being. When God looked upon man and saw that it was "not good that man should be alone" (Gen. 2:18), He made him a helpmeet. God commanded the man and his wife to be fruitful and replenish the earth. In response to this command, Adam and Eve brought forth children and the family was established. God also raised up other social groupings—tribes, nations, and the church. No man was to stand alone.

The sociality of the student points to the importance of the teacher's getting to know the student in terms of the various social relationships in which he participates. It also implies that Christian education programs need to train the student to live under the lordship of Christ in his family, church, school, and state. In this connection it should be observed that there is a grass roots concern for education in family living. Some church educators, I am thankful to say, have begun to respond to this concern. But we have only scratched the surface. So much more needs to be done in equipping students not only for family living but for every basic social relationship.

Another educational implication of the sociality of the student is the effect of interpersonal relationships on the learning process. A seventh grade history class, for example, is not simply a collection of individuals. There is an ongoing interaction between teacher and students and between student and students. The quality of fellowship within the class at any given time has a direct bearing on the quality of learning. This factor points to a very significant issue in educational theory. While all educators recognize the influence of interpersonal relationships on educational achievement, not all agree as to the nature and place of fellowship in the teaching-learning process.

On the basis of the Scriptural account of the origin of man

and the development of human institutions, it may be concluded that all men are created with a sense of need for human fellowship. Fallen man, however, with his man-centered view of life, attempts to meet this need in a fellowship that is horizontally formed—one established on the basis of the common interests of man as a sinner. Some examples of this type of fellowship include the old cronies that hang around the local bar, the Thursday evening poker club, or the group encounter session that is really nothing but a search for some new way to accept oneself without facing up to the sober reality of one's own sin and the need for repentance and faith in Christ.

Moreover, there is abroad today the belief that natural human relationships are the starting point for the discovery of life's meaning. This idea has found its way into the life of the church and has resulted in a de-emphasis on the preaching and teaching of the Scriptures. With regard to this current attitude, Lutheran educator Allan Hart Jahsman warned:

> He who maintains that "religion emerges from within the natural relationships of a child" and that "it is impossible to teach the Christian faith without the context of the Church" makes vertical relationships with God dependent on horizontal relationships with people instead of making interpersonal spiritual relations an extension of, a product of, personal Christian faith and at-one-ness with God.[13]

Jahsman goes on to say:

[13]Allan Hart Jahsmann, *What's Lutheran in Education* (St. Louis: Concordia Publishing House, 1960), p. 80.

to set forth a learning of the Christian faith and way of life through observation and experience in relationships per se, without adequately establishing the central role of direct instruction in the verbal revelation of God and personal life with Him, is to suggest a form of Christian pantheism in which truths and values are supposedly sensed apart from verbalization.[14]

He concludes

that interpersonal and group relationships are channels of the Holy Spirit (whether within the church or outside of it) only when they are avenues of Gospel communication.[15]

Of course, we must not minimize the importance of interpersonal relationships for the teaching-learning process. Rather, we need to recognize that (1) some distinction should be made between the context and the content of learning, and (2) the most fruitful environment for Christian nurture is a fellowship that has its origin, unity, and support in Jesus Christ. In other words, our fellowship must be vertically formed and sustained.

In a beautiful statement derived from the Scriptures, the Westminster Confession of Faith describes Christian fellowship in this way:

All saints, that are united in Jesus Christ their Head, by His Spirit, and by faith, have

[14]*Ibid.*
[15]*Ibid.*, pp. 80–81.

fellowship with Him in His grace, sufferings, death, resurrection, and glory: and, being united to one another in love, they have communion in each other's gifts and graces, and are obliged to the performance of such duties, public and private, as do conduce to their mutual good, both in the inward and outward man.[16]

As the people of God in any given educational setting come to a deeper knowledge of God as He has revealed Himself and His will in the Scriptures, their fellowship becomes all the more precious. This in turn provides the optimum environment for learning—one in which each individual is supported and encouraged as he ventures forth to learn some new dimension of truth.

The capacity for exercising dominion. When God made man, He gave him the task of subduing the earth and exercising dominion over all creation (Gen. 1:28, Ps. 8:6–8). To fulfill this cultural mandate man was actively to tame, cultivate, and utilize the animal, mineral, and vegetable resources that God had put into the universe for His own glory and for man's good. In thinking through the Scriptures as a whole, we can only conclude that Almighty God has made man, the one created in His image, to be responsible for serving Him as a faithful steward and obedient vicegerent in all the arts and sciences. What a singular honor! What an awesome responsibility!

As a result of the Fall, man lost his honored estate. He no longer possessed original righteousness. With his reason

---

[16]The Westminster Confession of Faith. Chapter XXVIII Par. 1, pp. 124–125.

darkened and his will perverted, he was no longer fit to dress and keep the Garden of Eden (Gen. 3:23,24). But through God's common grace man is still capable of marvelous achievements—raising crops, building cities, sending a man to the moon. Yet at the same time he pollutes the environment, squanders the natural resources, and somehow manages to corrupt every aspect of culture.

When Adam dressed and kept the Garden of Eden, he did so out of obedience to God. But when fallen man tills the soil, he acts out of self-interest. In so doing he develops a worldly and godless culture.

But in Christ man may not only recover what he lost in Adam; he may also be raised to a state of eternal glory. Redeemed by the cleansing blood of Jesus Christ and transformed by the renewing grace of the Holy Spirit, he has within him the wisdom, the love, and the power of God that enables him to obey the cultural mandate. "Where sin abounded, grace did abound more exceedingly" (Rom. 5:20). How amazing!

A consideration of man's ability and responsibility to subdue the earth and exercise dominion over all creation suggests a number of implications for Christian education. Only one, however, will be discussed here.

A very basic implication of the cultural mandate is that the church and school must recognize the complexity of what man must be taught. Education must be theoretical as well as practical. Man cannot exercise dominion over the world in which he lives if he is prepared merely to adjust to his environment, function efficiently, be good to his wife, his dog, and the mailman, and be able to work out his own income tax report. Thus functioning, he is no more than a cog in the wheel. For one made in the image of God, much more is required.

The Holy Scriptures teach that the faithful servant of Christ needs to study and reflect critically upon the cumulative heritage of the race. Only in this way will he be able to transcend mentally his environment and bring it under this dominion, even as he himself has been brought under the sovereign will of God. Thus the liberal arts, including language, literature, philosophy, history, science, mathematics, music, and art, are an essential component of the curriculum and should occupy more of the student's time and attention than any other area of study except the Scriptures. Furthermore, inasmuch as the cultural mandate was given to all men, liberal arts should be required of every student to the degree consistent with his ability and vocational calling.

THE PROBLEM OF SIN

All men are "dead in trespasses and sins" and are "by nature children of wrath" (Eph. 2:1,3). Although the unregenerate man may know the truth in a relative sense and thus succeed in developing the arts and sciences to a high degree, he cannot think God's thoughts after Him and thus cannot know anything truly. Moreover, he is not able to develop a civilization that is honoring to God and fulfilling to himself. Therefore, the deepest need of every human being (and in the context of education, every learner) is to be brought into a right relationship with God.

How is this to be accomplished? If a lack of knowledge were the problem, then more education would be the answer. Of course, the problem is much more serious. As a sinner, man is spiritually blind and deaf, and as long as he does not have "ears" to hear and "eyes" to see, no amount of training—even training in the Bible—will make him anything more than an educated pagan. There must be a radical change in man. As Jesus declared: "Except one be born anew, he cannot see the kingdom of God" (John 3:3).

Regeneration, however, is wholly the work of God (John 1:12). The Christian minister or educator cannot quicken those who are spiritually dead. Only the Holy Spirit can do this

(Eph. 2:1; Col. 2:13). Nevertheless, to the extent that God uses the knowledge of the Gospel and the knowledge of one's sin in the internal calling of the sinner and in preparing him for conversion, man may be involved in the teaching-learning process. Herein, the Christian educator, motivated by a fervent desire to see all those entrusted to his care come to salvation, may be an instrument in the hands of God as he teaches the glorious Gospel of Jesus Christ.

Another educational implication of the sinful condition of man is that discipline must be administered. Because man is not good by nature, contrary to the contention of non-Christian educators, he cannot be left to his own devices. He will not, if left completely unrestrained, develop into a model of virtue. Even the "born again" learner needs the support of Christian discipline, that is, discipline exercised in a manner agreeable to the Scriptures. Parents and teachers, therefore, ought to take care to establish sound rules and regulations—few in number and biblically grounded—and then consistently enforce them. Of course, this must be done out of Christian love, but it must be done.

How then should the teacher view the student? This chapter as a whole is an attempt to answer that question, and I can think of no better way to sum up what has been said than to quote these words of the Dutch educator Hylkema:

> Honor the child; honor God's laws operative in him; honor God's purpose, and behold even in the most ragged youngster the eternal possibilities that lie enwrapped in his soul, and only in this way will God honor us and deem us fit and worthy to lead that child in the green pastures and to open for him the way to a fuller life.[17]

---

[17]G. W Hylkema, "The Great Office of the Teacher in Preparing the Child for the Complete Life" in *Fundamentals in Christian Education* ed. by Cornelius Jaarsma (Grand Rapids: Wm. B. Eerdmans Publishing Company, 1953), p. 419.

3

THE COVENANT OF GRACE AND THE CHRISTIAN EDUCATION OF COVENANT CHILDREN

"Hear, O Israel: Jehovah our God is one Jehovah: and thou shalt love Jehovah thy God with all thy heart, and with all thy soul, and with all thy might. And these words, which I command thee this day, shall be upon thy heart; and thou shalt teach them diligently unto thy children, and shalt talk of them when thou sittest in thy house, and when thou walkest by the way, and when thou liest down, and when thou risest up." (Deuteronomy 6:4–7)

The doctrine of the covenant of grace has received little emphasis in recent times even among those confessionally committed to covenant theology. This neglect of an invaluable part of our theological heritage has left the Reformed community in some measure theologically disoriented in the practical application of faith to life. Nowhere has this been more evident than in the dichotomy we have made between what we profess to believe in our creeds and what we actually do in the nurture of our children. Professor Louis Berkhof put it this way:

In the American ecclesiastical world the doctrine of the covenant is almost entirely unknown . . . Moreover, it is quite evident that in most of the churches of our land, even in those who theoretically subscribe to the doctrine of the covenant, the doctrine has no grasp on the life and the conscience of the people in general, and fails utterly to have a determining influence on the education of their children.[1]

These remarks made more than a quarter of a century ago are just as true today.

One example is the paucity of material written on the subject. Imagine a visit to your local Christian bookstore. As you look around the store, in all probability, you will see a large space devoted to books on the Christian family dealing with various aspects of husband-wife and parent-child relationships. A number of these books will be given to special problem areas such as pre-marital sex, barriers to family communication, and parent-teenager conflicts. Only very rarely, however, will there be a book on the parental nurture of children and rarer still a book which attempts to work out the implications of the covenant of grace for the nurture of covenant children.

The problem is further illustrated by the apparent lack of understanding of the meaning of covenant membership. A young couple present their infant son for baptism in the regular Sunday morning worship service. They are beaming with pride. Smiles of approval can be seen throughout the congregation. What a cute baby! After a few introductory remarks, the minister asks the couple the following questions from *The Book of Church Order:*

---

[1]Louis Berkof, "The Covenant of Grace and Its Significance for Christian Education," in *Fundamentals in Christian Education,* ed. Cornelius Jaarsma (Grand Rapids: Wm. B. Eerdmans Publishing Company, 1953), p. 20.

(1) Do you acknowledge your child's need of the cleansing blood of Jesus Christ, and the renewing grace of the Holy Spirit?

(2) Do you claim God's covenant promises in (his) behalf, and do you look in faith to the Lord Jesus Christ for (his) salvation, as you do for your own?

(3) Do you now unreservedly dedicate your child to God, and promise, in humble reliance upon divine grace, that you will endeavor to set before (him) a Godly example, that you will pray with and for (him), that you will teach (him) the doctrines of our holy religion, and that you will strive, by all the means of God's appointment, to bring (him) up in the nurture and admonition of the Lord?[2]

After each question the couple routinely answers in the affirmative. But do they really understand the questions addressed to them? Does the congregation understand? The minister? From this writer's own experience and from numerous conversations with people representing a large segment of several denominations, it may be concluded that for all too many these questions are given very little thought. How easy it is to participate mindlessly in a ritual as familiar, as beautiful, and as sweet as the baptism of a baby.[3]

What does it mean to be a member of the covenant? What

[2]*The Book of Church Order of the Presbyterian Church in the United States* (Richmond, Virginia: The Board of Christian Education, The General Assembly of the P.C.U.S.), pp. 204-5.

[3]Many churches who do not believe in the practice of baptizing infants have instead a public service of child dedication. For additional information and a suggested order of service see Zegler, Franklyn M. *The Broadman Minister's Manual* (Nashville: Broadman Press, 1969), pp. 113-117. "This service," as Segler points out, "is actually a promise of parents to offer their child (usually in infancy) to God, and to dedicate themselves to the rearing of the child to the glory of God" (p. 113).

are the privileges and obligations of membership? If believers and their children are members of the covenant, what difference does this make in the way Christian parents are to educate their children?

Perhaps a good place to begin is with a brief review of the biblical grounds for the doctrine of the covenant of grace.

THE BIBLICAL DOCTRINE
OF THE COVENANT OF GRACE

The one story of the Bible is the story of a relationship, one which God Himself established with a people chosen from among every tribe and tongue and from every time and place and with whom He made a covenant, a covenant of grace. In Genesis 17:7-9, there is this very precise and formal statement of the covenant:

> And I will establish my covenant between me
> and thee and thy seed after thee throughout
> their generations for an everlasting covenant,
> to be a God unto thee and to thy seed after
> thee. And I will give unto thee, and to thy seed
> after thee, the land of thy sojournings, all the
> land of Canaan, for an everlasting possession;
> and I will be their God. And God said unto
> Abraham, And as for thee, thou shalt keep my
> covenant, thou, and thy seed after thee
> throughout their generations.

Throughout the Scripture there is one covenant of grace. The promises, prophecies, and sacrifices in the Old Testament point to the birth, life, death, and resurrection of Jesus Christ in the New Testament. The fulfillment is better than the promise, the reality better than the shadow (Hebrews 8-10), but the covenant in the Old and New Testaments is essentially the same. It has the same promise—"I will be thy God" (Exod. 6:7; 2 Cor. 6:16–18; Rev. 21:3). It proclaims the same plan of salvation—"Abraham believed God, and it was reckoned unto him for righteousness" (Gen. 15:6; Rom. 4:3). It is based upon the work of the same mediator—"For there is one God, one mediator also between God and men, the man Christ Jesus" (1 Tim. 2:5). It has the same membership, namely, believers and their children—"For to you is the promise, and to your children" (Acts 2:39).

THE STATUS OF THE CHILDREN
OF BELIEVING PARENTS

The very fact that children of believing parents are members of the covenant and others are not suggests that there is something different about their status before God. But what the difference is is the question, for quite obviously the answer we give will have a direct bearing on the way we educate our children. Unfortunately, the differences among Reformed theologians on this issue have tended to complicate the problem for those who are concerned with the Christian nurture of covenant children.

Some theologians have taken the position that children of believing parents should be presumed to be regenerate.

Lewis B. Schenck, for example, in his book *The Presbyterian Doctrine of Children in the Covenant,* contends that children of believing parents should be treated as though they were already Christian. In this connection, he writes:

> Granting, however, that the church does have many in its number who are not Christians, yet it is likewise true that she should not receive anyone into the church except those who presumably are Christians. Our judgment then must be a judgment of charity. We must

38

take the position that those who profess their faith in Christ as their personal Saviour are presumably Christians. Likewise, we must accept the children of believing parents as presumably God's children, on the basis of the covenant promise of God. In the first instance, the ground of such belief is profession of faith; in the second instance, the covenant promise of God. One is certainly no less a ground for assurance than the other. In either case those who enter the church on these grounds are presumably God's own children.[4]

In another place Schenck quotes with approval Dr. J. W. Alexander:

... ought we not daily to say (in its spirit) to our children, 'You are Christian children, you are Christ's, you ought to think and feel and act as such!' And, on this plan carried out, might we not expect more early fruit of the grace than by keeping them always looking forward to a point of time at which they shall have new hearts and *join the church?*[5]

According to this point of view, the task of the Christian educator is to nurture the Christian life already begun. This is a very appealing position, especially to a professional Christian educator. He may begin Christian nurture at the birth of the child. There is no need to put off religious instruction until

[4]Lewis B. Schenck, *The Presbyterian Doctrine of Children in the Covenant* (New Haven: Yale University Press, 1940), p. 11.

[5]*Ibid.*, p. 81.

after a conversion experience. The child may be brought up in an orderly way learning more and more what it means to be a child of God.

The theory that covenant children are to be treated as though they are already Christian, however, is not without some rather difficult problems. The promise of God is not unconditionally given to all the seed of Abraham. Paul makes this very clear in Romans 9:6–8:

> For they are not all Israel, that are of Israel: neither, because they are Abraham's seed, are they all children: but, in Issac shall thy seed be called. That is, it is not the children of the flesh that are children of God; but the children of the promise are reckoned for a seed.

Thus the children of God (those who are elected to eternal salvation) are called from within a chosen people (the entire membership of the covenant). In the history of redemption the inner group has sometimes been larger, sometimes smaller, but there has always been a remnant. All members of the covenant receive the promise of salvation and participate in the benefits of the covenant in much the same way that all Israelites benefited from being members of the commonwealth of Israel. Salvation, however, becomes a reality only in the lives of the elect (Romans 9:11). We can and should, therefore, treat all children of believers as members of the covenant with all the privileges and obligations this entails, but we cannot and should not treat all children of believers as though they were already Christians at birth, and thereby neglect our most solemn responsibility to lead them to Christ.

Sometimes those who favor the idea of presumptive regeneration cite the example of John the Baptist, who being filled with the Holy Spirit, leaped in his mother's womb for joy at the approach of Mary bearing the Savior in her womb (Luke 1:15, 41,44). But, it must be pointed out, what was true of John the Baptist is certainly not true of all members of the covenant (Romans 9:13). Moreover, the experience of John the Baptist does not necessarily apply even to all elect members of the covenant. The Scripture gives us a basis for determining the order of regeneration in the plan of salvation (John 3:3; Ephesians 2:1–10; 1 Corinthians 2:14), but it does not give grounds for fixing the time of regeneration in a person's life. It may take place in the mother's womb, or it may occur much later, accompanied by the teaching and preaching of the Gospel. We simply do not know.

It is sometimes also said: "Just as we presume the adult believer to be regenerate, we presume the child of believing parents to be regenerate. We do not actually know that either are regenerate but we have as much grounds for the one as we have for the other."

But is this really a valid comparison? We are forced to make a presumption about the adult who professes belief only because we cannot know his heart. We would not hesitate to say on Scriptural grounds that if the adult is a true believer in Jesus Christ, he is regenerate. On the other hand, we cannot make the statement on Scriptural grounds that if a child is born of parents who truly believe we know the child is spiritually reborn. True believers without exception are born again. Children of believers may or may not be. A presumption about the former, therefore, does not justify a presumption about the latter.

Should we then take the opposite position that covenant children are to be presumed unregenerate and that they cannot profit from Christian nurture until they have been converted? Should the Christian community approach the children of believers in the same way as the children of non-believers? If so, what then is the advantage of membership in the covenant?

41

Quite obviously there are practical advantages to living in a Christian home where the Word of God is taken seriously. The child of believing parents has opportunities to learn what it means to be a Christian in ways not available to the child of unbelieving parents. But this is not the issue. The question really comes down to this: Are there inherent advantages for the child of believing parents by virtue of his status as a covenant child? Are there benefits for him that go beyond his being in greater proximity to the Word?

The answer is an emphatic yes! First of all, as a member of the covenant, he is an heir of the promise God made to His people when He said: "I will be their God, and they shall be my people" (Jeremiah 31:33). It may be helpful to pause there briefly and urge the reader to consider just how precious a promise really is—that is, a promise that is made by one who has both the intention and the ability to keep it. For instance, a father promises his eight year-old son that he will buy him a bicycle for Christmas. The son knows that his father is a man of integrity and that he has the means of keeping the promise. He lives therefore each day in the expectation that this promise will be fulfilled. If the father had not promised to buy his son a bicycle, he, of course, could have bought it for him anyway, but he would not have been obligated to do so nor would the son have had any basis for expecting it of him. So then, it is no little matter that God has made His people a promise, especially one so awesome and glorious as the promise to be their God.

It is important at this point to distinguish between being an heir of the covenant promise and an heir of salvation. The former suggests the need for claiming the content of the promise; the latter does not inasmuch as it is presupposed that the content of the promise is present at birth. Pierre Marcel put it this way:

> . . . children born in the covenant are *heirs*. But their heritage is *that of the promise,* of which

the Holy Spirit is the pledge. We can never insist too much on this point in opposition to those who obstinately maintain that according to us the heritage has to do with salvation. These children do not inherit salvation and eternal life. Salvation is not hereditary! They inherit only the promises. It behooves them thereafter to receive the *content* of the promise by faith and repentance, and thus by regeneration and conversion, and to live a life consecrated to the Lord. Then, and then only, will they be heirs *of the things promised.* The heritage is only communicated to the heir who receives the promise *with faith.*[6]

According to this view the advantage of the covenant child is not in the presumption of his salvation but in the assurance of his privilege as an heir of the promise together with his corresponding obligation. The attitude of the Christian community toward the child of believing parents, therefore, is that he is an heir, an heir of God, and the question of regeneration is left in the hands of God. The basis for the nurture of the covenant child does not rest upon his present spiritual condition, but on the command of God. The presumption is that if God has commanded that covenant children be brought up in the nurture and admonition of the Lord, He will enable the child to benefit from this instruction. This teaching may then culminate in a genuine repentance from sin, a saving faith in Jesus Christ, and a life self-consciously lived under the Lordship of Christ.

---

[6]Pierre Marcel, *The Biblical Doctrine of Infant Baptism* (London: James Clarke and Co. Ltd., 1953), pp. 107–108.

The question is sometimes asked: "Should we try to convert the covenant child or should we train him as though he is already in the process of sanctification?" The tension suggested by this question is based on the erroneous assumption that the Christian education of covenant children must be grounded on the presumption that they are either saved or lost. It can be said, of course, on the grounds of logic, that the child is either born again or that he is not, but it cannot be said that Christian parents are thereby forced into using a training program that has an uncertain foundation. As Christian parents we can fulfill our obligations resting on certainties. We know that the child of believing parents is a member of the covenant (Genesis 17:7, Mark 10:14, Acts 2:39). We know also that the covenant child is to be trained in all that is involved in being a Christian—becoming a Christian as well as all that comes thereafter (Deuteronomy 6:4–7, Psalms 78:5–6, Ephesians 6:4). The Christian parent does not wait until he is certain that his child is born again before he teaches him to be holy, to pray, to acknowledge that all he is and all he has belongs to God. Neither does he wait until his child comes to the age of discretion before he explains to him in ways appropriate to his maturity that he is a sinner and that he needs to repent and believe. From the very beginning of life the child of Christian parents is taught by precept and example to claim the precious promise ("I will be their God") and fulfill the solemn obligation ("they shall be my people") of membership in the covenant of grace.

SOME BASIC PRINCIPLES FOR THE
CHRISTIAN EDUCATION OF COVENANT CHILDREN

Having a child is one of God's greatest blessings. As the Psalmist has said: "Lo, children are a heritage of Jehovah; and the fruit of the womb is his reward. As arrows in the hand of a mighty man, so are the children of youth. Happy is the man that hath his quiver full of them: They shall not be put to shame when they speak with their enemies in the gate" (Psalms 127:3-5).

My first child, a daughter, was born thirty years ago in a small county hospital about 11:30 P.M. I was allowed to stand just outside the delivery room door. Hearing my infant daughter make her first sounds, I knew right away that her lungs were in excellent condition. After a time the nurse wrapped her in a blanket and brought her into the waiting room. I took my daughter in my arms and for the first time I really knew what it was like to be a father, and I have been learning ever since.

The birth of my second child, also a daughter, has helped me to understand the uniqueness of the human personality. How is it possible that two children could have the same parents and essentially the same environment and yet be so different? When I stop to think about it, it is extremely difficult to say exactly in what particulars they are different. One thing is certain—they are both very unpredictable. Let me hasten to say that both of my children, each with her own distinctive personality, as they were growing up sometimes made me delight in their presence, and sometimes, quite honestly, made me want to climb the wall. Nevertheless, through the years they have fully confirmed the Psalmist's statement: ". . . children are a heritage of Jehovah" (Psalms 127:3).

Having a child is a great blessing. It is also an awesome responsibility. The home more than any other institution influences the child for good or evil. Basic attitudes, habits, and values are developed during those early formative years when the child is almost exclusively under the care and direction of the family. Proverbs reminds the parent of this obligation and opportunity with these words of wisdom: "Train up a child in the way he should go, and even when he is old he will not depart from it" (Proverbs 22:6).

The Christian parent, giving thanks for his children and accepting his parental responsibility, needs to know how to educate his "heritage from the Lord." Before setting forth the specifics of the day-by-day training of children, however, I would like to present a few basic principles for the purpose of giving direction in the use of instructional methods. These principles may be stated as follows:

The authority and responsibility for the training of children is delegated primarily to the parents. It was to the parent that the command was given: " . . . provoke not your children to wrath: but bring them up in the nurture and admonition of the Lord" (Ephesians 6:4, KJV).

Two words in this passage are singled out for special consideration. The first word, "nurture," translated from *paideia*, means "the upbringing and handling of the child which is growing up to maturity and which thus needs direction, teaching, instruction and a certain measure of compulsion in the form of discipline or even chastisement."[7] The second word, "admonition," translated from *noutheous* denotes "the word of admonition which is designed to correct."[8] The two terms taken together in the context of Ephesians 6:4, as I understand it, mean the direction, instruction, and correction in righteousness that Jesus Christ gives through the parent to the child in bringing up the child to maturity so that he self-consciously lives the whole of life under the Lordship of Christ, which includes bringing up his own children "in the nurture and admonition of the Lord."

The primary objective of the Christian parent is to bring up his child to maturity so that he is equipped to glorify God in every area of life. At the end of the great doctrinal section of

[7]Gerhard Kittel, ed., *Theological Dictionary of the New Testament*, Vol. V (Grand Rapids: Wm B. Eerdmans Publishing Company, 1967), p. 596.
[8]*Ibid.*, Vol. IV, p. 1021.

Romans, Paul gives a beautiful doxology which concludes with these magnificent words: "For of Him, and through Him, and unto Him, are all things. To Him be the glory forever. Amen" (Romans 11:36). The chief end of life is also the chief end of education.

The goal is not that the individual merely be able to recite the words, "The chief end of man is to glorify God," but that he come to the point, through Christian nurture, where in the depth of his being and in every situation he actually glorifies God.

Subsumed in this comprehensive objective are these absolutely essential goals: to lead the child to a saving knowledge of Jesus Christ; to help the child see himself as he really is—not as the center of the universe but in relation to God as the center of the universe, not as one to be ministered unto, but as one to minister; and to train the child as God's vicegerent in exercising dominion over the world in which he lives.

Because there has been some confusion about the use of the phrase, "exercising dominion over the world," a few words of explanation may be in order here. By "exercising dominion" it is simply meant that the individual Christian is actually involved in reforming culture so that it is honoring to God. It is, I am sure, easy to see that when a Christian farmer, in response to God's command to subdue the earth (Gen. 1:28), develops a procedure to raise more food per acre, he is exercising dominion. This would be equally true inother professions or trades such as law, medicine, carpentry or for that matter, in any cultural activity. In a similar manner, when a child is brought up to Christian maturity, establishes his own home, and brings up his children in the nurture and admonition of the Lord, he is, in a very biblical sense, exercising dominion.

The methods of instruction should be consistent with the nature and theological standing of the child. It may seem obvious to most people that children and adults cannot be taught in the same way, especially as to the depth and breadth of the material to be covered, but in actual practice this distinction is often overlooked. Moreover, following the same principle, allowances should be made for the various stages of development through childhood.

This is indeed a Scriptural teaching. Proverbs 22:6a is literally translated: "Train up a child according to his way." I understand "his way" to mean the child's nature as a child. This means that the training of the child is to be in such concert with his level of maturity that what is taught is so imprinted on his heart and mind that it becomes his second nature, and thus always remains with him. In harmony with this interpretation, Franz Delitzsch, regarded by evangelicals as one of the greatest of the Old Testament commentators, translated Proverbs 22:6a in this way: "Give to the child instruction conformably to his way; so he will not, when he becomes old, depart from it." In this commentary on the verse, he wrote:

> The instruction of youth, the education of youth, ought to be conformed to the nature of youth; the matter of instruction, the manner of instruction, ought to regulate itself according to the stage of life, and its peculiarities; the method ought to be arranged according to the degree of development which the mental and bodily life of the youth has arrived at.[9]

If the truth of Proverbs 22:6 were actually observed, we would avoid the extremes of either underestimating or overestimating the learning capacity of the child. Anyone who works with small children is constantly amazed at their ability

---

[9]Franz Delitzsch, *Biblical Commentary on the Proverbs of Solomon,* Vol. II (Grand Rapids: Wm. B. Eerdmans Publishing Company, 1968), pp. 86-87.

to learn. Certainly children must be encouraged to use their full potential. On the other hand, there should be no attempt to pressure very young children to learn heavy doctrine presented in a very abstract form or to make decisions for which they are not prepared. In the long run this can only hinder their progress.

The marvelous thing is that there is no contradiction between God's will as revealed in the Scripture and His will as observed in the laws of child growth which God Himself has ordained. The spiritual progress of the child, therefore, is best promoted when the learning of the child is directed in a manner agreeable to those laws as we are enabled to understand them in the light of the Scripture. God's truth taught to His children in accordance with their way is His way. And on His way we cannot improve.

MEANS OF CHRISTIAN NURTURE

How is the Christian parent then to fulfill his covenant responsibility to train his children in the ways of Christ? Let me suggest four ways.

Discipline. First of all, parents must discipline their children. Discipline should not be thought of as a coordinate of nurture, but is in itself a means of nurture inasmuch as it enables the child to understand more fully the righteousness of Christ. But it must be rightly handled. The discipline which the Christian parent administers to the child must be that which the Lord prescribes. The nature, purpose, and means of discipline should be according to His will.

Discipline, for example, should never have as its purpose making a person worthy of acceptance in the kingdom of God. Salvation is by grace, not of works. Christ Himself paid for the sins of those who belong to Him (Romans 3:24–28). Surely we cannot add anything to the finished work of Jesus Christ.

Neither should discipline aim to get even with one's children

49

for causing one to lose face. At first thought the very suggestion that anyone would do this may seem very unlikely, even repulsive.

Consider the following not so hypothetical example. Mrs. Jones has a five year-old daughter whose name is Sandy. Last Sunday Mrs. Jones and Sandy sat together at church during the morning worship service. Early in the service Sandy began to squirm, makes faces at other children when she could get their attention, and even ocassionally say something that could be heard two pews away. All of Mrs. Jones' whispered admonitions were to no avail. Mrs. Jones felt that every eye was focused on them. She was so embarrassed. Later at home out of ear shot of her fellow parishioners, Mrs. Jones gave Sandy a severe tongue lashing followed by a vigorous spanking. There is no doubt that Sandy deserved correction. The question is, why did Mrs. Jones do it? Was it to administer justice, was it for the benefit of the child, or was it to satisfy the demands of her own inner frustration? Was it, in effect, getting even with the child?

As one imperfect parent to another, I will have to confess that my motives are not always as noble as I would like for them to be. Nevertheless, discipline should always aim to correct the child so that he can grow as a servant of the Lord Jesus Christ. This will require the wise and prayerful use of various means.

First of all, at a very early stage, boundaries should be set as to what the child may or may not do. They should be Scripturally grounded, few in number, clearly defined, appropriate to the age and maturity of the child, and consistently enforced. For example, if the parent for valid reasons establishes 8:30 P.M. as the time his child is to be in bed on week nights, he should insist on this being done unless there is some legitimate excuse for not doing so. If the rule is enforced consistently for a week or two there will come a time when the child will not ground him from the activities that have prevented him from doing his school work, such as television on week nights until his grades take a turn for the better. If he is hard to get up in the morning, let him sleep and suffer the consequences, such as missing breakfast or having to walk to school.

What about the use of the rod? For the contemporary humanist, this is a relic of a more primitive time. The humanist cannot conceive of a humane person resorting to this form of punishment. He simply cannot understand how a method which for him is dehumanizing may be used to humanize a person in the true sense of that term.

The Christian parent, on the other hand, takes seriously the biblical teaching: "He that spareth his rod hateth his son: But he that loveth him chasteneth him betimes" (Proverbs 13:24 KJV). In applying this admonition it would be my understanding that this form of discipline should be used wisely, never in anger, and always in love. Ordinarily it should be reserved for young children on the occasion of serious disobedience and administered only after explanation has been given as to the reason for this action. But it should be used whenever necessary.

It should be noted that discipline includes verbal instruction as well as correction through chastisement. From the very beginning the child should be taught right behavior. As the child grows and matures he should be more and more internally disciplined by his knowledge of the truth. This is, of course, the goal of the Christian parent. He wants his child to be mature in Christ, able to exercise self-discipline, motivated by a sincere love for God, and directed by His Word.

Personal example. Secondly, parents must teach their children the blessings and responsibilities of the covenant life through their own personal example. A cursory reading of the Epistles of Paul reveals the importance the Apostle placed on personal example as an essential means for the elders to teach

51

have to be made to go to bed at the time that has been set. Occasionally the child may test the parent to see if the boundary is still there, but if he is shown that it is, he will realize that he must plan his activities within that boundary and act accordingly.

The consistent enforcement of boundaries actually enables the child to enjoy the full measure of his freedom as a responsible covenant child. It gives him a sense of security in knowing where the limits are. In this connection, James Dobson tells this very interesting story:

> During the early days of the progressive education movement, one enthusiastic theorist decided to take down the chain-link fence that surrounded the nursery school yard. He thought the children would feel more freedom of movement without that visible barrier surrounding them. When the fence was removed, however, the boys and girls huddled near the center of the play yard. Not only did they not wander away, they didn't even venture to the edge of the grounds.[10]

This is one way to help the child understand that the blessed freedom of the covenant is through joyful obedience to God.

When chastisement is administered it should be appropriate for the kind of wrong behavior. If the child has been carelessly playing pitch and catch with the neighborhood playmate in the living room and accidentally breaks a vase or window, let him pay for the damage out of his allowance. If he has fallen down on his grades because of not spending enough time studying,

---

[10] James Dobson, *Dare to Discipline* (Wheaton: Tyndale House Publishers, 1970), p. 56.

their flock the way of God (2 Thess. 3:9, 1 Tim. 4:12, Titus 2:7, 1 Peter 5:3). The same holds true for parents. We cannot expect to teach our children to love, trust, and obey God truly unless we ourselves truly love, trust, and obey God. Our children are not likely to exhibit the quiet and meek spirit becoming to a child of God unless they see in us an authentic and transparent faith.

The Christian life style of the parents helps to provide a home environment which is instrumental in the development of the child's religious beliefs. A loving human father who prays daily with his family is likely to facilitate the child's understanding of a loving heavenly Father. The child who experiences the warm embrace of a Christian mother when he is hurt or afraid is better prepared to understand the goodness of God and to know what it means when the Scripture says: "As one whom his mother comforteth, so will I comfort you. . ." (Isaiah 66:13).

Even as an infant the child should be present in family worship so that from the very beginning of his life he is exposed to the reality of God as a personal Being. The reality of the concept of a personal God must, of course, be further developed in the context of a Christian home in which the parents and the older children live each day solving problems, fulfilling obligations, and making plans for the future in such a manner that it is completely obvious that for them God is real and Christ is Lord. Gideon Yoder quotes an unknown source as reporting that John Paton, the great missionary, once said: "God was so real to my father that He became real to me."[11]

Situational teaching. Thirdly, parents must inculcate in their children a living faith through what might be termed situational teaching. No institution has as great an opportunity to seize upon life situations that occur in such varied relationships and circumstances and turn them into profitable learning experiences (Ephesians 5:16) as has the home. When children get into an argument, when a choice has to be made as to where the family will spend their vacation on a limited budget, when a member of the family suddenly becomes ill, parents should view these situations not simply as problems to be solved or crises to be faced but as occasions to teach their children how to apply the Christian faith to their everyday life.

Perhaps the most opportune situation for Christian instruction is when the child asks a question. He is never more ready to hear the content of the faith. Numerous examples of this type of teaching are found in the Scripture. Exodus 12:26–27 is a case in point. When Moses commanded the children of Israel to observe the passover, he included this special exhortation to parents: "And it shall come to pass, when your children shall say unto you, What mean ye by this service? that ye shall say, It is the sacrifice of Jehovah's passover, who passed over the houses of the children of Israel in Egypt, when he smote the Egyptians, and delivered our houses."

When the child asks a question he should be given a thoughtful answer. Most Christian parents will be very careful to give the child a biblical answer. Sometimes, however, they may forget to answer the child in terms of his maturity. A three year-old boy who was accustomed to hearing me preach from a high pulpit and seeing me dressed in a long black pulpit gown came up to me one Sunday morning following the worship service and confronted me with this question: "Is you God?" After I had had time to recover from the shock of such an unexpected question, I stooped down and put my hand on his shoulder and said: "No, I am not God, but I am His servant. God is here at the church and he is also where you live." Now, a three year-old is not able to understand all the attributes of God. He is, however, able to understand that there is a distinction between God and a minister of God and that God's presence is not limited to the sanctuary of a church. In a similar manner, the parent is continually helping the child to grow in a sound understanding of the faith by gently correcting wrong ideas while at the same time providing true information.

Children have a way of getting right to the heart of a matter and asking questions that would overwhelm a learned theologian such as: Where did God come from? Who made God? What was the nationality of Adam and Eve? Most often the Christian parent will be able, in his own way, to provide a suitable answer. If, however, he is unable to answer the question, he should be honest and simply confess that he doesn't know. Parents are not required to know everything. This may be a good time to relate the child more closely with the church by enlisting the aid of the pastor or an elder in answering the question.

Planned teaching. Finally, the Christian parent should carefully plan for the nurture of his children. He should see to it that they are receiving sound instruction in a church school and also, if possible, in a Christian day school. Christian nurture ideally conceived requires a close cooperation of home, school, and church.

At night when the child is in bed, the Christian mother or father should plan to take a few minutes to sit down beside him, talk to him, share with him, and pray with him. These moments at bedtime also provide an excellent time for telling Bible stories.

Telling a Bible story requires careful preparation. The Bible story should be read through several times and then told in one's own words. The parent should ordinarily keep the Bible open in his hands while telling the story so that the child is visually reminded that this is from the Word of God.

Young children like to hear a Bible story repeated. Our youngest daughter, for some reason, frequently asked to hear the story of Philip and the Ethiopian eunuch. This is not unusual. Repetition helps a child to learn, so when the child asks for a favorite Bible story, it is good to tell it to him again.

As the child grows older and learns to read he will enjoy reading Bible stories as well as other kinds of Christian literature. The adolescent may enjoy and profit from reading classics such as *Pilgrim's Progress* and biographies of great Christians such as John Calvin and Martin Luther. Christian literature appropriate for all ages should always be readily available in the Christian home.

One-to-one verbal teaching is an essential part of family nurture. The child ought to be reminded of the promise that God has made to him as a member of the covenant. In this connection, the parent should share with his children what Christ means to him and how He has worked in his life. The means of grace—such as baptism, for example—ought to be explained carefully. Concerning his baptism, Matthew Henry said:

> I cannot but take occasion to express my gratitude to God for my infant baptism: not only as it was an early admission into the visible body of Christ, but as it furnished my parents with a good argument, and I trust, through grace, a prevailing argument, for an early dedication of myself to God in my childhood. If God has wrought any good work upon my soul, I desire, with humble thankfulness, to acknowledge the influence of my infant baptism upon it.[11]

We have delineated a number of methods for the purpose of trying to clarify the task of Christian nurture. But in a real sense these methods cannot be mechanically separated. They are interrelated and constitute a pattern of nurture that exer-

---

[11]Gideon G. Yoder, *The Nurture and Evangelism of Children* (Scottdale, Pennsylvania: Herald Press, 1959), p. 175.

cises a formative influence upon the child from the very beginning of life.

For the Christian family that takes its responsibility seriously, the usual and normal procedure is to take the child's sorrow for particular sins, such as lying or cheating, and develop it into a sorrow for and repentance of sin as a mark of rebellion against God; to take his incipient faith and nurture a life of trust in Christ and grateful obedience to His will. Although every person must come to that time when he self-consciously repents of his sin and commits his way to Christ, it is quite likely that for the child of a Christian home this will be the culmination of a nurturing process and will not necessarily be attended by a marked crisis experience. The child brought up in an authentically Christian home in which all the means of grace have been faithfully used in the nurturing process may be able to say truly in adulthood, "I can never remember the time when I did not know and love the Lord Jesus Christ."

4

THE CHRISTIAN SCHOOL:
AN INSTITUTION WHOSE TIME HAS COME

*". . . and He is before all things, and in Him
all things consist. And He is the head of the
body, the church: who is the beginning, the
firstborn from the dead; that in all things He
might have the preeminence."* (Colossians
1:17–18)

In ever-increasing numbers Christian parents are turning to
the Christian school as a way of educating their children. As
long ago as 1967, Bob Brown and Henry Buchanan, in an article in *Christianity Today*, predicted that if the enthusiasms for
the Christian school were to continue unabated, there would
come a time when the Protestant Christian school would take
its place alongside the Roman Catholic school and the public
school as a third force in American education.[1] Admittedly it is
difficult to obtain reliable figures on the actual growth rate of
the Christian school movement. Some schools belong to more
than one association. Others operate independently of all professional groups. State education authorities have a tendency
to lump all non-public schools together. Thus it is impossible

---

[1] Henry A. Buchanan and Bob W. Brown, "Will Protestant Christian Schools
Become a Third Force?" *Christianity Today* 11 (May 12, 1967), p. 3.

to make an accurate assessment of the extent of the increase of Christian schools. Nevertheless, competent observers agree that over the past two decades there has been substantial growth, and that at least in some measure the Protestant Christian school has already become a third force in American education.

The growth of the Christian school has brought with it both agreement and disagreement, ardent support and severe criticism, and evangelical Christians have taken stands on every side of the issue. Nevertheless, an institution that is likely to have such a significant impact on the educational scene merits serious consideration by all thoughtful Christians. What has brought about the Christian school movement? What makes a school Christian? If the Christian school is an essential institution, who has the responsibiity for organizing and supporting it? These and other questions will be discussed in this chapter.

ITS ORIGIN

Factors that have contributed to the educational crisis. There are many factors, varied and complex, that have contributed to the disastrous situation in which modern public education finds itself today. Let me point out three of the most obvious ones.

First of all, consider the gradual secularization of the public school. In colonial America, much of education was self-consciously influenced by the Protestant Reformation. The seeds of universal education had been sown by the Reformers. Luther, Calvin, and others proposed such great doctrines as the priesthood of all believers, the authority of the Scripture, and justification by faith alone, all of which made necessary the education not only of the clergy, but also of the laity. If the Bible and the catechism were to be put in the hands of every boy and girl, then every boy and girl must have at least a basic education.

This motivation was evident in the early public school legislation. In 1642 the General Court of Massachusetts passed a law which in effect required parents to see to it that their children could read and understand the "principles of religion and the capital laws of the country."[2] A portion of the Massachusetts Act of 1647 declared:

It being one chief object of that old deluder, Satan, to keep men from the knowledge of the Scriptures, as in former times by keeping them in an unknown tongue, so in these latter times by persuading from the use of tongues, that so at least the true sense and meaning of the original might be clouded by false glosses of saint-seeming deceivers, that learning may not be buried in the grave of our fathers in the Church and Commonwealth, the Lord assisting our endeavors,

It is therefore ordered, That every township in this jurisdiction, after the Lord hath increased them to the number of fifty householders, shall then forthwith appoint one within their town to teach all such children as shall resort to him to write and read. . .

It is further ordered, That where any town shall increase to the number of one hundred families or householders, they shall set up a grammar school, the master thereof being able to instruct youth so far as they may be fitted for the university.[3]

[2]As quoted in Newton Edwards and Herman G. Richey, *The School in the American Social Order* (Boston: Houghton Mifflin Co., 1947), p. 56.
[3]*Ibid.*, pp. 62-63.

The earliest public school textbooks also demonstrated this interest in Christianity. The most widely used textbook in colonial times was the *New England Primer*. It contained the alphabet illustrated by a series of rhymed couplets which were mostly drawn from the Scripture. For example, it began, "In Adam's fall, We sinned all," and ended with, "Zaccheus he, Did climb the tree, his Lord to see." It also included prayers, hymns, catechisms, the Lord's Prayer, church creeds, the Ten Commandments and short sermons. In a large measure the public school in early New England was an instrument of the Christian community.[4]

As our society became more and more religiously heterogenous the existence of the public schools was threatened. How could a school in a large urban community be acceptable to the people as a whole when they came from such diverse religious backgrounds? One can sympathize with those who were faced with such a dilemma. By the middle of the nineteenth century it was evident that leaders from both the educational and the political sectors would attempt to resolve the problem by the removal of sectarian elements from the curriculum. This was done, but it did not happen overnight. The process of secularization went on for more than a century. Today, at least in a legal sense, the process is complete. In 1953 the American Council on Education declared: "Public education in the United States is committed by federal and state law to the general principle that sectarian religious instruction must be excluded from the curriculum."[5] Recent court decisions and state and federal laws unfavorable to the use of the Bible and prayer in the classroom were not the beginning of the process

---

[4]Christopher J. Lucas, *Our Western Educational Heritage* (New York: The Macmillan Company, 1972), p. 478.

[5]Committee on Religion and Education, *The Function of the Public Schools in Dealing with Religion* (Washington, D.C.: American Council on Education, 1953), p. 1.

of secularization, as some have believed, but rather the end result of it.

The course taken by the public school over the past century and a half has been based on the idea that education is religiously neutral. This, of course, is an impossibility. As has already been pointed out, we can separate church and state, but we cannot separate religion and education. The ultimate end of education, the nature of the persons educated, the nature of truth—all these are religious questions requiring religious answers. The answers may issue from the religion of secularism or humanism, or they may issue from the religion of Christianity, but they will be religious answers. In this sense, every school—public or private, Christian or non-Christian —is a religious school actively involved in the teaching of religion. The question for the Christian parent is not whether or not he wants his child taught religion in school but whether he wants his child taught Christianity or some other religion.

Almost a century ago, Dr. A. A. Hodge, the great Princeton theologian, made these almost prophetic remarks:

> It is capable of exact demonstration that if every party in the State has the right of excluding from the public schools whatever he does not believe to be true, then he that believes most must give way to him that believes least, and then he that believes least must give way to him that believes absolutely nothing, no matter in how small a minority the atheists or the agnostics may be. It is self-evident that on this scheme, if it is consistently and persistently carried out in all parts of the country, the United States system of national popular education will be the most efficient and wide instrument for the propagation of Atheism

which the world has ever seen.[6]

To present a totally anti-Christian picture of public education would be unfair and inaccurate. We must not overlook the faithful work of many Christian teachers, administrators, and board members in the public schools, as well as those Christian officials in various state departments of education. God has not left Himself without a witness in the academic arena. We pause to give thanks for this. At the same time, it must be understood—make no mistake about it—that the program, the curriculum, and the objectives of public education are officially committed to a secular position, which is inescapably a religious position.

A second factor that has contributed to the educational crisis is the lack of quality in public education. In 1973 an estimated "19 million Americans over 16 were functionally illiterate," according to a *New York Times* article.[7] Functional illiteracy is understood to mean the inability to read well enough to meet the needs of everyday life, such as reading the newspaper, filling out a job application, or taking an examination for a driver's license. Moreover, the *Times* claims that "The general decline is hardly limited to the slums. . . . Achievement has also dropped among students from districts with more affluent homes."[8]

In the light of the amount of money the nation now spends on public education ($70.7 billion for primary and secondary

[6]A. A. Hodge, *Popular Lectures on Theological Themes* (Philadelphia: Presbyterian Board of Publication and Sabbath-School Work, 1887), p. 281.

[7]Frank E. Armbruster, "The More We Spend, The Less Children Learn," *The Compact New York Times Magazine* (New York: Arno Press, Inc., August 28, 1977), pp. 81-82.

[8]*Ibid.*, p. 83.

education[9]—as much as $4,000 per child annually in some school districts),[10] it is difficult to blame the problem on inadequate funding. On the contrary, the evidence suggests that there is no correlation between the amount of money spent and the level of academic achievement.

The decline in academic performance has been accompanied by a significant increase in school vandalism, physical assault, drug abuse, and other types of destructive and disruptive behavior. In some cases schools are indeed "blackboard jungles" in which teachers and students fear for their personal safety. Senator Birch Bayh, who served for six years as Chairman of the Senate Subcommittee to Investigate Juvenile Delinquency, reported that the Committee's nationwide survey of 757 school systems shows school vandalism and violence to be increasing in frequency and intensity. "In some schools," Senator Bayh said, "the problems have escalated to a degree that makes the already difficult tasks of education nearly impossible."[11]

A graphic way of illustrating the extent of school violence and vandalism is by its cost. In 1974 when the Los Angeles school system was facing a $40 million deficit, $7 million had to be diverted from its education budget for vandalism prevention and repair. According to the National Association of School Security Directors, in 1972 more money ($590 million) was spent for school vandalism-related costs than on school textbooks on a national level.[12]

The root cause for the lack of quality in education is religious in nature. There is today in the public school a

[9]George E. Jones, "On Opening Day America's Schools Ponder Some Sobering Lessons," *U.S. News and World Report* 83 (September 12, 1977), p. 29.

[10]Armbruster, *op. cit.*, p. 81.

[11]Birch Bayh, "Seeking Solutions to School Violence and Vandalism," *Phi Delta Kappan* 59 (January 1978), p. 300.

[12]*Ibid.*, p. 301.

spiritual vacuum. The lack of a unifying purpose inevitably brings with it a pervasive sense of meaninglessness, hopelessness, and despair. The ideal of educating the whole man, which has been the rallying cry of the progressive educator for most of this century, never really had the whole man in mind. Even educational reformers such as Charles Silberman who recognize that the crisis in education "grows out of a new and growing concern with the quality of life . . . that man does not live by bread alone,"[13] nevertheless interpret the problem and project the solution as though man is earth-bound—as though he has no soul. It is a question of the blind continuing to lead the blind from one crisis to another.

Finally, we would be less than candid if we did not admit that some of the adverse reaction to the public school has not been because of the poor quality of education, nor the secularization of the school, but because of court-ordered integration, forced busing, and other political and social factors. The sudden change in the ratio of one race or ethnic group to another cannot help but be disruptive, at least in the beginning. The fact that we are reaping the consequences of the sins of the past and perhaps also of the present does not alter the adverse effects of the break-up of the neighborhood school. In this situation it would be very easy for anyone interested in the development of private schools to exploit the fear and dissatisfaction of public school patrons for their own ends. Furthermore, it is entirely possible that some parents are placing their children in Christian schools more out of a desire to escape integration than from a heartfelt commitment to Christian education. These issues are very real and must be faced honestly and thoughtfully by all proponents of the Christian school.

[13]Charles E. Silberman, *Crisis in the Classroom* (New York: Random House, 1970), p. 22.

The public response to the educational crisis. The response to the educational crisis of which I speak has been varied. Many people have remained very loyal to the public school and have been outspoken in its support. These advocates write books, place large ads in local newspapers, and organize conferences urging people to rally around the public school. Some with this point of view almost instinctively connect the public school with the preservation of the American way of life—which has become, in a manner of speaking, a substitute religion. Thus, to bring into question the public school by setting up private schools in competition with it is considered un-American and even sacrilegious. For these people the public school is sacrosanct and must be promoted at whatever cost.

Others support the public school but for very different reasons. They are quite aware of the secularization of the school, the drug abuse, the number of unmarried teenage mothers, and the climate of violence, and they are deeply disturbed. But as Christians they feel burdened to penetrate culture, including the public school, and witness to it. This concern is biblically based. The Christian cannot live in a partitioned society; in order to be "the salt of the earth" and "the light of the world" he has to go where the action is. There are some questions here, however, that must be raised. Should we give a Christian teacher who asks whether or not he should teach in a public school the same answer we would give to a Christian parent who asks whether or not he should place his children in a public school? Is the Christian's responsibility limited to bearing witness to culture or is he also obligated to serve as an instrument for the reformation of culture?

In ever-increasing numbers, people have turned to some form of private education as a way of accommodating themselves to the current educational crisis. Some have established private schools that differ very little in philosophy, textbooks, and curriculum from the public schools from which they came.

Such private schools differ from public schools only in that they are segregated rather than integrated, thus continuing a cultural tradition which they regard as important. When race ceases to be an issue in education, the private non-sectarian segregated school will have no reason for existing. Indeed, in a number of areas where racial tensions have eased, this type of school has already had to close its doors.

Other private schools have been established with the intention of remedying some of what are perceived to be existing problems in the public school. For example, in many metropolitan areas at least one of the private schools is set up for the purpose of returning to the basics of education: the emphasis on phonics in the teaching of reading; the emphasis on the classical studies; the return of foreign languages, the sciences, and ancient history to the curriculum; the upgrading of discipline; and the reinstatement of high standards for grading, all of which to them are very important. To those of us in the academic community who have been so turned off by the anti-intellectualism and permissiveness of progressive education, this approach may seem to be a much more palatable option. And yet this model has to be considered more carefully. Classical humanism may come in more attractive dress than contemporary humanism—although this observation is in the eye of the beholder—but underneath there is the same rebel. As long as the basic education type of school is man-centered in its approach, it already contains the seeds for producing the same kind of institution from which it has withdrawn.

In addition, many people have established private schools with the sincere desire to identify them in some way with the Christian faith. What frequently happens, however, is that Christian practices such as worship and Bible instruction exist alongside the educational program without actually being integrated with it. Required Bible classes and chapel services do not in and of themselves make a school Christian. Ownership and administration of a school by a church or a Christian parent society does not make a school Christian. A school with a secular educational program and with only a coating of Christianity is not in the truest sense Christian and furthermore is very vulnerable to the onslaught of anti-Christian forces at work in the world today.

Is there not some better way for the Christian parent? I believe there is.

The deep conviction of this writer is that the Christian school in which faith and learning are integrated is the most viable alternative for the Christian parent in the midst of our current educational crisis. Such a school is not perfect, for the simple reason that fallible people make up the faculty, student body, administration, and patron's society. Educators in the Christian school still make many of the same mistakes they made in the public school, and children still misbehave, antagonize the teacher, and commit all manner of mischief. Sin is in the Christian school just as it is in the marketplace. There is a difference, however—a decided difference. The people in a Christian school for the most part take the Lordship of Christ seriously, and this makes a radical difference in that entire academic community. Here the love of Christ and the truth of Christ make an impact on the total life style of the child every day. As an institution, the Christian school is the most consistent implementaton of a Biblical world-and-life view as it is applied to the education of children in today's complex society, which is marked by such a high degree of cultural differentiation.

WHAT IS A CHRISTIAN SCHOOL?

The Christian school defined. A school is an academic community. A Christian school is a Christian academic community with the distinctive task of equipping students individually and corporately to exercise dominion in Christ over all that He has made. Some additional comments on each element of the above definition may be helpful.

A community is a body of people living and working together under the same laws. A Christian community is a body of people living and working together under the authority of the Scripture. They are bound together by a commitment to one greater than self. As they are drawn out of themselves unto Christ they are drawn to each other in a fellowship unlike any other fellowship. This community provides the essential context for education.

A Christian school is an academic community in that it is involved in the process of schooling. A Christian school cannot be truly Christian without being truly a school. In some cases the "Christian school" has received a bad reputation because it uses class time primarily for evangelism and devotional teaching, having little or no regard for academic work. Every Christian, of course, including the Christian teacher, is always concerned about making disciples for Jesus Christ. There is no conflict here between the cultural mandate and the Great Commission. But there is a time and a place for everything. The school is not a church, and a history class is not simply an occasion for another devotional message. The Christian school receives students with a wide range of academic abilities from a wide variety of socioeconomic backgrounds and should offer them the highest quality of true education. Nothing less can be done in the name of Christ.

The task of exercising dominion in Christ entails taking that which God has made and forming and shaping it into a culture—agriculture, education, government, law, medicine, art, technology, commerce, etc.—so that it is honoring to God. In the fulfillment of this task the school obviously has to take into consideration the maturity, gifts, and calling of the student. No individual can do everything, but the child of God can be taught to bring himself and all that has been entrusted to him into subjection to the Lord Jesus Christ.

The essential characteristics of the Christian school. There is great diversity among Christian schools because there is great diversity among Christians and also among the cultures in which the schools are located. There is no mold from which all of them must be stamped. Schools that are truly Christian, however, all have in common a faithful adherence in theory and practice to the teaching of Scripture. This common factor may be broken down into three essential characteristics:

A faculty that translates a Christian philosophy of education into everyday classroom practice. To say that there can be no Christian education without Christian educators is to say the obvious. What is not so apparent is that there can be no Christian education without the application of a Christian view of teaching and learning. Christian teachers do not automatically put into practice a Christian philosophy of education. It is not surprising that some Christian teachers, having been trained in secular professional schools and having been culturally conditioned to divorce Christianity from the arts and sciences, are likely, for example, to believe in their hearts that the pupil is made in the image of God but in actual practice to deal with him as though he were only a higher form of animal life. This situation produces an impossible tension between faith and practice and between practice and the reality of the learning process.

On the other hand, Christian teachers should not become discouraged if they do not perfectly implement a Christian philosophy of education even after much effort has been put forth. I have frequently had teachers come to me, after hearing me lecture on this topic, and say, "I believe that what you are saying is true, but I fall so far short of the ideal that I feel like throwing up my hands and quitting." After quickly explaining that I also fall short of the ideal, I go on to point out that, like sanctification, putting into practice a Christian philosophy of education is a lifelong process. As a headmaster of a Christian school I knew that I was not apt to find very many teachers who were well-trained in a Christian world-and-life view, and fewer still who could put it to use in a significant way in such matters as the integration of faith and learning. I did believe, however—and my experience has confirmed this—that I could find authentic Christian teachers who were willing to work with each other and with me in trying each day to apply our faith to our task as Christian educators. The realization that religion cannot be compartmentalized, that it has a bearing on all of life including that which we do in the classroom—the teaching of subject matter, the exercise of discipline, and the evaluation of student progress, for example—is a major breakthrough and is the beginning of a lifelong adventure in bringing every aspect of our profession into subjection to the Lord Jesus Christ. And that makes the difference between a school that is Christian and one that is not.

A dynamic and integrated curriculum that is theocentric in its orientation. There is an age-old controversy between those who advocate a content-centered approach to education and those who advocate an experience-centered approach. The Experimentalist says, "We must teach the child. His felt needs are the most important factor to be considered and should be the organizing principle of the curriculum." The Classicist responds, "We must train the student to think, to use his mind. The quicker we get back to those subjects that will help the student discipline his mind, the better off we will be." The former absolutizes man's experience. The latter absolutizes man's reason. Both absolutize man.

Content or experience, is that the question, or is there another alternative? From a Christian perspective there is indeed another approach—a God-centered approach. But isn't this simply the manipulation of words? How can there be an approach that is neither content-centered nor experience-centered? The answer is a curriculum that is shaped by the

71

Word of God, a norm that transcends both the content of the arts and sciences and the experience of the individual learner. In this way neither content nor experience is absolutized. The cumulative experience of the race as well as the particular experiences of the individual stand under the judgment of Scripture. Only from this vantage point can a curriculum be designed that will truly reflect the structure of knowledge and at the same time adequately provide for the real needs of the student.

A God-centered curriculum is of necessity an integrated curriculum. All the diverse areas of knowledge, including the content of the curriculum, have their unity in God, who is the source of all truth. The curriculum, therefore, ought to reflect this divinely ordained diversity and unity. Each course of study should be a distinct area of instruction and yet essentially interrelated with every other course of study.

My observation has been that the curriculum of the typical Christian school is very much like that of the public school with the exception of a required Bible course. In all fairness, however, this is one of the most difficult problems to solve, even by those most committed to the philosophy of education expressed in this book. Much more research needs to be done.[14] Meanwhile there is much that a school can do. It may be helpful to start with an area of study such as the language arts, which are more easily integrated. Interdisciplinary assignments may be used. The faculty in a given school can read selected books that give a Christian interpretation of a subject area and then discuss with each other how this discipline may be integrated with other disciplines. And, of course, all Chris-

[14]Works such as *Shaping School Curriculum: A Biblical View,* edited by Geraldine J. Steensma and Harro W. Van Brummelen, and *Joy in Learning* by Arnold H. De Graaff and Jean Olthuis are very helpful in stimulating more thought in this direction.

tian educators, not just a few scholars, need to be involved in the research referred to above.

A God-centered curriculum is also subject to revision. To be sure, God is unchanging. He is "the Father of lights, with whom can be no variation, neither shadow that is cast by turning" (James 1:17b). "His truth endureth to all generations" (Psalm 100:5b, KJV). However, God has so made man that there is always the possibility of his developing a deeper understanding of the truth and of finding new applications of it in different situations and in each succeeding generation. Moreover, the search for new dimensions of the truth that God has written into the very fabric of the universe is a never-ending human activity. (A good illustration is the contemporary emphasis on the exploration of outer space.) For this reason the curriculum must always be open for the inclusion of new materials and the reexamination of the curriculum as a whole in the light of the Scripture.

The truth in its wholeness—for the whole child, for the whole of life, for the glory of God—this is what the curriculum is all about.

An administration that directs school policy as one under Divine authority. The integrity of the Christian school is absolutely essential. When a school is operating on a very limited budget, as most Christian schools are, its very life is seemingly affected by the patron's willingness to keep his child in school and pay his monthly tuition. This makes the school very vulnerable to the whims of any patron who is especially vocal. The particular form of sponsorship—parent society, church, private ownership, etc.—makes no difference; the temptation is the same.

The school, therefore, must continually remind itself of what it is and for Whom it ultimately exists. In this regard it is very helpful to have a constitution, adopted by the sponsoring body, that recognizes the supreme authority to whom both the sponsoring body and the board of trustees are responsible and

73

that grants the board authority to administer the school in its day-to-day operations subject only to annual review by the sponsoring body.

When a patron says to a headmaster, "I pay tuition each month to send my child to this school; therefore, I ought to have the right to have my child excluded from certain requirements, if that is my wish," the headmaster ought to be able, with the full support of the board, to respond, "We very much want to operate the school in such a way as to merit the approval of all our patrons. Nevertheless, it would be unfair to exempt your child from that which is required of all other students. We really want your approval, but even more we want the approval of the One who brought the school into being and who continues to sustain it. Your money buys something very precious. It buys the best Christian education we are able to provide for your child. It does not buy special privileges that result either in unsound educational practices or in injustices for others."

An administration—board, headmaster, principal—directing school policy as one under authority has the obligation to be consistently Christian in all administrative tasks, including the setting of goals, the employment and supervision of teachers and staff members, the recruitment and oversight of students, the development of the curriculum, the methods by which the school is financed, and the school's relationship to the community. Even the concept of administration should be rooted and grounded in the Scripture.

One cannot conceive of a school as defined and described above apart from a standard of excellence. God asks the very best from those who would serve Him. This obligation to excellence extends to the total program and requires each person involved in the teaching-learning process to work up to the level of his ability.

WHY DO WE NEED A CHRISTIAN SCHOOL?

There are still many people, especially those who live in the "Bible belt" of the United States, who have available to them a public school in which at least some of the teachers are professing Christians and the discipline is reasonably good as measured by today's standards. Why then, it is asked, should I sacrifice in order to put my child in a Christian school? Why not send my child to a public school for which I am already paying taxes?

In responding to this question a number of factors that could be held up in favor of the Christian school readily come to mind. It usually has a higher quality of education, smaller classes, a more favorable teacher-student ratio, and an atmosphere relatively free of violence and vandalism. The real reason for the Christian school, however, goes much deeper. At the most basic level the Christian school is essential because of the religious nature of education and because of the cultural aspect of education.

The religious nature of education. Reference has already been made to the fact that although all education is religious, not all education is Christian. The choice is between a Christian religious education and a non-Christian religious education. If this is true, there are no material circumstances that can justify a Christian parent in giving his child an education that is man-centered and thus dishonoring to God. Would you send your child to a Buddhist shrine to worship because it was nearer your home or because it was already paid for by the state? Of course not! Then we can say with equal certainty that we cannot send our children, in the most formative years of their lives, to be shaped religiously by a non-Christian religious educational institution.

The cultural aspect of education. The decree that God gave to man to subdue the earth and exercise dominion over it (Gen. 1:28, Psalm 8:6ff.) has never been repealed. The fall of man seemed to preclude the fulfillment of this mandate. Yet the Scripture assures us that one day it will be accomplished through Christ (Heb. 2:8). Education of the redeemed man in Christ, therefore, is never complete, never adequate, until he is prepared to see the world, history, science, literature, social institutions, and his own life through the eyeglasses of the Scripture and is thus informed to help shape his environment, family, profession, art, business, and government to conform to the teachings of God's revealed will.

But who will do this? What institution is equipped to provide this kind of education? The institutional church calls us to repent and believe and builds us up in the faith. It prepares us in very foundational ways for our cultural task. But it is not the church's primary mission nor is it the church's particular competence to acquaint us in an analytical sense with our cultural heritage.

The Christian family is charged to bring up its children "in the nurture and admonition of the Lord" so that when they are adults they can in turn bring up their children in the same way (Eph. 6:4, Psalm 78:5–6). In a primitive society it was possible for parents to train their children for their cultural tasks. Even at the beginning of this century it may have been possible for a well-educated parent to have taught his children adequately the various disciplines then included in the curriculum of the local school. Today, however, when we have experienced what some have called a "knowledge explosion," this practice would be very impractical for most families, whatever the extent of their educational background.

Consider, for example, what it would be like for a parent to sit down in the evening after a full day at the office or factory and teach his children, ranging in ages from eight to eighteen, various subjects from mathematics and physics to geography, taking into account the present level of complexity of each field, and interpreting it all from a Christian point of view. Obviously the family needs help, the kind of help that specialists could give to assist them in this task.

What is needed, then, is a Christian school as an extension of the family (not a substitute for it) and as a partner of the church. The religious nature of education points up the need for a Christian rather than a public or "non-sectarian" private school. The cultural aspect of education underscores the need for a school to complement the educational ministry of the church and family.

HOW THE CHRISTIAN SCHOOL
SHOULD BE CONTROLLED

The issue here is: who is responsible for the education of covenant children and, having determined that, what form of school control is required?

Responsible agency. Historically the responsibility for the education of covenant children has been assumed primarily by the family, church, state, or some combination of these three. In Geneva, Calvin succeeded in welding together state, church, and family to provide instruction for the people as a whole. Today those that follow Calvin face a very different situation. Given our present religious pluralism and complex culture, what should be the responsibility of the family, church, and state in the education of children?

The family. The prior right and obligation of the parent to educate his children is a well-attested Scriptural teaching. Children are a gift of God to the parents and are to be regarded by them as one of God's greatest blessings (Psalm 127:3–5). The authority of parents is implied in the fifth commandment: "Honor thy father and thy mother, that thy days may be long in the land which Jehovah thy God giveth thee" (Exod. 20:12). The duty of children is to "obey your parents in the Lord: for this is right" (Eph. 6:1).

Parents are exhorted to teach their children the law of God

(Deut. 6:4–7), and "to bring them up in the nurture and admonition of the Lord" (Eph. 6:4b, KJV). Children are admonished to "hear the instruction of thy father, and forsake not the law of thy mother" (Prov. 1:8).

That the home has primary authority in the education of children is clear and generally recognized among evangelical Christians. Moreover, evangelicals are basically of one mind that the church has an interest in the education of children and that the state has at least some regulatory powers. What is not so clear and generally agreed to is the extent of the educational responsibility of the church and state.

The church. Norman DeJong, who has made a very helpful contribution to educational philosophy, in defending his position that the education of covenant children is the exclusive responsibility of the family, interprets the teaching function of the church as being limited to the unregenerate. Commenting on Matthew 28:19, he writes:

> The disciples, as leaders in the church, were directed, to "teach all nations, baptizing them."
> The clear implication is, then, that the message of the church of Christ is a call to teach the Truth of God to the *unregenerate.* (Italics mine.)[15]

In the view of this writer, the implication drawn by DeJong from his passage is not clear at all. The Greek word *mathēteuō* which DeJong translates "teach" is probably better translated "make disciples of." This does indeed refer initially to the unregenerate. But the Great Commission does not end here. It goes on to say in verse twenty: "teaching (*didaskontes*) them to observe all things whatsoever I commanded you." Here the

---

[15]Norman DeJong, *Education in the Truth* (Philadelphia: Presbyterian and Reformed Publishing Co., 1969), pp. 125-126.

present tense of the participle "teaching" denotes continuous action and cannot be limited to the pre-baptism experience of the unregenerate. As Philip Schaff points out:

> The *teaching* is a continuous process, which partly precedes baptism, as a general exhibition of the gospel with the view to bring the adults to the critical turning point of decision for Christ, and submission to His authority, and partly follows baptism, both in the case of adults and infants, as a thorough indoctrination in the Christian truth, and the building up of the whole man unto the full manhood of Christ, the author and finisher of our faith.[16]

Again using the Great Commission as the basis of our discussion, one cannot discern a body of content to be taught exclusively by the church. Parents as well as the church teach the commandments of our Lord (Deut. 6:4–7, Psalm 78:5–6). Nor are there any exegetical grounds in this passage for excluding children from the teaching ministry of the church. A careful examination of other relevant passages such as Acts 5:42 and 11:26 yield similar conclusions. How then can we distinguish between the educational responsibility of the church and the family? And perhaps equally important, how may they be related so that they complement rather than compete with each other?

The church is primarily concerned with its members as a whole; the parent is primarily concerned with his own children.

---

[16]John Peter Lange, *Commentary on the Holy Scriptures,* Vol. 8 (Grand Rapids: Zondervan Publishing House, 1960), p. 558. See also R. D. Culver's paper on Matthew 28:16–20 in the *Bulletin of the Evangelical Theological Society* 10 (Spring 1967), pp. 115-126.

The church is equipped through its offices and government (Acts 15:1–35, Eph. 4:11ff.,[17] 1 Tim. 3) to proclaim the gospel to the sinner, to build up the saints in the faith, and to help the people of God to bring the perspective of faith to every area of life. The parents are equipped through their special relationship with their children (Gen. 1:28, 17:7–9; Psalm 127:3) and through family government (Eph. 6:1–4) to help them put their faith to work in the practical affairs of everyday life. The educational responsibilities of the family and church overlap. They differ in terms of degree and overall institutional purpose.

The overlapping of educational responsibility and the complementary character of institutional purpose suggest the necessity of close cooperation while the integrity of each institution is maintained. On this basis the covenant community through the instituted church has an obligation to stand with the covenant family in carrying out its covenantal task. This includes encouragement, prayer, financial support, and even the setting up of a school, if necessary, as long as the school and church are not integrated (i.e., expansion of the offices of the church to include schoolmaster, or teacher) and the overall purpose of the church or family is not compromised.

A study paper presented to the General Assembly of the Presbyterian Church in America raised the question, "But if the church becomes involved in parochial education does that mean that she has invaded the parent's realm and has done what the government, today, is doing in its public (government

---

[17]Calvin interpreted pastor and teacher in Eph. 4:11 to be two separate offices rather than two functions of one office. He applied the office of teacher not only to the teacher of theology but also to the teacher of arts and sciences. It is my view that Eph. 4:11 is talking about two functions of one office and refers to an ecclesiastical *office*.

controlled) education?"[18] and then gave its answer, "We think not as long as the parental assignment is preserved and encouraged."[19] I concur with this judgment, but would like to add, "and as long as the integrity of the institutional church is 'preserved and encouraged.' "

The state. As it has already been pointed out, education is rightly the special province of the parent and in a more general sense the business of the church. The state can justify its entrance into education only on the grounds that the family and church have abdicated their responsibility. Interestingly enough, the state's gradual takeover of education has always been accompanied by an acquiescence on the part of the parents and the church. This is a very sad part of the history of American education. If the Christian community objects to the state's overwhelmingly dominant role in education today, in large measure we have ourselves to blame.

The state does, however, have a legitimate role to fulfill. It is responsible for the administration of justice and the promotion of the public good (Rom. 13:1–4). In this capacity the state has the right and the obligation to see to it that the student is housed in a safe building in an environment conducive to good health and that he is provided with an education of such quality as to enable him to be functionally literate in today's world. This latter obligation suggests two areas of special concern on which further comment is needed.

First of all, does the state, in the administration of justice, have the right to require parents to send their children to school? It is my view that it does. Some object to compulsory education on the ground that the child belongs to the parent

---

[18]"Report of the Christian Education and Publications Committee to the Sixth General Assembly of the Presbyterian Church in America," *Commissioner's Handbook for the Sixth General Assembly of the Presbyterian Church in America* (Calvin College, Grand Rapids, Michigan, June 19-23, 1978), p. 704.
[19]*Ibid.*

and not to the state. This is true, but certainly the parent's special relationship with the child cannot be interpreted to mean that he has an arbitrary power over him. Just as the parent does not have the right to exploit or abuse his child, neither does he have the right to deprive him of an education. Others object to compulsory education on the ground that it would give the state authority to force parents to send their children to public schools. This does not necessarily follow. The state could compel parents to educate their children without compelling them to do it in any prescribed way. We have to distinguish between compulsory education and compulsory public education. Compulsory education, yes! Compulsory public education, never!

Secondly, does the state within the scope of its divinely ordained function have the right to accredit schools? Again, it seems to me that in protecting the rights of the parent and the child the state may establish accreditation standards as long as these standards do not in any way coerce the school to compromise its Christian commitment. The state accrediting authority, for example, has the right to require a private Christian school to have written objectives and an educational strategy designed to meet those objectives. It is not the state's prerogative, however, to define the objectives or to specify the educational strategy to be used. If the state should abuse its authority and encroach upon the rights of the parent to provide his children with a Christian education through a private school, at this point the sponsoring body of the school has no other choice but to "obey God rather than men" (Acts 5:29), and be willing to suffer the consequences.

Form of control. How then can we organize a school so that its form of control is consistent with the way in which responsibility has been assigned? In order to answer this question we proceed to a brief evaluation of some of the best known forms of control now being used by non-public Christian schools, including the parent society school, the parochial school, the individually owned school, and the independent board-controlled school.

The parent society school. This type of school is owned and operated by the parents who have organized for this purpose. Theoretically only the children of believing parents are admitted. Historically the Christian Schools International (formerly the National Union of Christian Schools) has supported this form of control. Dr. Mark Fakkema, one of the founders of the N.U.C.S. and a staunch advocate of the parent society school, reasoned:

> The Home has certain inalienable rights. Among these is the right to train its own children. To train one's own offspring is not only a Divine right but it is also a divinely imposed duty. We hold that in so far as the parents cannot personally discharge their educational obligations they should carry out their educational responsibility jointly with other parents holding basic views of education similar to theirs. This can be done by the parents forming a Christian school society.[20]

This type of school has an illustrious history, especially among those who belong to the Christian Reformed Church. It focuses attention on the responsibility of the parent. It is defended on the grounds of covenant theology, to which I am personally committed. The parent society school is certainly a legitimate option. With all due respect, however, I question whether or not it is mandated by the implications of covenant

---

[20]Mark Fakkema, "The Organization of the Local Parent-Society Christian School Plant," *Course of Study for Christian Schools* (Grand Rapids: Wm. B. Eerdmans Publishing Co., 1947), p. 369.

theology. The parent society is not the same as the individual parents who make it up. The whole cannot be equated with any individual part of the whole. When the parent sends his child to a parent society school he is delegating his responsibility in much the same way he would be doing if he were sending his child to a parochial school or an independent board-operated school. If the parent is exclusively responsible for the education of his children and if he cannot delegate this task to an agency outside the family, then, to be absolutely consistent, only the parent himself or a tutor directly under his control could educate his children. And if the parent could actually do this he would not need a school in the first place.

There is also a practical problem with the parent society school. There is no built-in system of maintaining the theological emphasis of the original parent group that established the school. My own limited observation has been that as additional parents are added through the years there is a tendency to dilute the theological basis upon which the school was formed. This is especially true in those areas where the parent society is not reinforced by ethnic and ecclesiastical ties.

The parochial school. As the name implies, this is a school that is owned and operated by the institutional church. It will usually admit the children of anyone who will agree to their children being educated under the religious teaching of the sponsoring church. The parochial school is the most numerous type of non-public school, and the Roman Catholic Church has by far the largest parochial school system, to the extent that it is often thought that the parochial school is by definition a Roman Catholic school. This form of control follows from their view that the right "to educate belongs preeminently to the Church."[21]

---

[21]Pope Piux XI, *Christian Education of Youth,* as quoted in *Selected Readings in the Philosophy of Education,* ed. by Joe Park (New York: The Macmillan Company, 1958), p. 306.

The parochial school, however, is not necessarily based on this rationale. There are other reasons why this form of control is used. The Missouri Synod Lutheran Church, which has probably been more active than any other Protestant denomination in fostering this type of school, is a case in point. This denomination believes that the parents have the primary but not exclusive responsibility for educating their children, and that they may discharge their obligation either through the church or apart from it.[22] The decision to establish or not to establish a parochial school, for them, apparently comes down to whether or not to do so is in the best interests of the Kingdom of God. A. C. Stellhorn, a Lutheran educator, put it this way:

> The question for us is not: Who is obligated to provide a general education? but: What is best for the Kingdom of God? How can the Christian Church as an organization best perform the work instituted by Christ for the salvation of sinners? This basic consideration has indicated, and always will indicate, a complete Christian education for Christians and all others who will accept it, for the sake of the individual and the State as well as the Church.[23]

Lutheran belief, then, makes the parochial school optional rather than mandatory. Practically speaking, however, the Lutherans have most often adopted this form of control.

The parochial school in some form is for many people, particularly in communities where people are not bound together

---

[22]Jahsmann, *op. cit.* p. 27.
[23]*Ibid.*, p. 37.

by strong cultural ties, the easiest type of school to establish and maintain. In addition, it provides a ready-made structure through which the covenant community can give needed assistance to the covenant family in carrying out its educational responsibility, a responsibility it cannot adequately fulfill on its own in today's world. A parochial school provides a stable situation for schooling. It is more difficult to dilute the theological basis of this type of school. Nevertheless, a school so directly under the control of the church is always tempted to forsake its academic character and prepare students more for the church than for life as a whole. The church sometimes, too, runs the risk of allowing the school (one in which faith and learning are not integrated) to compromise its primary mission.

The individually owned school.[24] This type of school is owned and operated by a sole proprietor. There is no board. It is operated for profit. The advantage of this type of school is that decisions can be made quickly without anyone being consulted (although this can also be a disadvantage). The original theological position that brought the school into being is not likely to change. The profit motive is an incentive to be efficient and to offer the best product in a competitive market.

This school's strength may also be its greatest weakness. So much depends upon one person. What happens when the individual dies or becomes incapacitated? The sole proprietor type of school also does not facilitate the close cooperation of church, family, and school, which is a prerequisite for a sound program of Christian nurture. There is also something more to be said about the profit motive. As praiseworthy as it may be,

---

[24]For a well-known example of this type of school see Robert L. Thoburn, *How To Establish and Operate A Successful Christian School* (Fairfax, Virginia: Fairfax Christian School, 1975), especially pp. 16-17.

it is not the only motive that can move a person to be efficient. Whatever the secondary considerations, the Christian's primary motive must always be his desire to serve one greater than self—the Lord Jesus Christ (Col. 3:23–24). When a work is unto Christ, it is done from the heart. We do not scheme to get by with the irreducible minimum of either effort or cost, but we use every possible means as efficiently as possible because it is a work that we offer to Christ.

Independent board-operated school. This is a school owned and operated by a self-perpetuating board of directors. It may take many forms. My own experience in organizing a Christian school has been with a non-profit corporation. In our case the board of directors was made up of the elders of our church plus the board of trustees of the school. (I selected the original board of trustees, but of course it doesn't have to be done in this way.) There was some overlapping here because some of the elders were also trustees. The board of directors elected the board of trustees whose terms were set up on a staggered basis. The month-by-month operation of the school was under the direction of the board of trustees subject to an annual review by the board of directors.

This system worked very well for us. The fact that the elders of the church were also members of the board of directors made for close cooperation between church and school. There is here, however, the problem of the school being more removed from the parents than would be the case in a parent society or parochial school. We tried to compensate for this by practicing an open-door policy to all the parents and encouraging an active patron's society.

Obviously we have no revealed form of control and none can be absolutized. Each one that has been worked out over the years in the experience of the Christian community has its strengths and weaknesses. I do believe, however, on the basis of what has been said in this section, that we can come to the following conclusions:

1. Parents should choose the most authentic Christian school available to them. The form of control, though very important, is not crucial.
2. The covenant community through the institutional church should support the covenant family in fulfilling its educational responsibility. This may or may not include the establishing of a parochial school.
3. The integrity of the church, family, and school must be maintained.

With this in mind I personally could support some form of the parent society, parochial, or independent board-operated school. The way each of these is implemented is more important, in my judgment, than the form itself.

Those of us who are committed to the Christian school have to attend to much unfinished business before our vision can become a reality. We need to develop graduate programs to train professional educators and to provide a climate for research; we need to write textbooks for the curriculum of the elementary and secondary schools, and professional literature for teachers and administrators; and we need to develop a financial structure that includes the Christian community as a whole, as well as the parent, so that the Christian school does not become an elitist school ministering to only one segment of society. This is our task. God has given us the resources and the opportunity. The time is at hand to move forward.

As we observe a greater and greater polarization between good and evil, between Christ and the world, with so many forces competing for the minds and hearts of our children and of people in general, is it not possible that God has raised up the Christian school to take its place alongside the Christian church and the Christian family for a time such as this? I believe with all my heart that He has!

5

FROM SUNDAY SCHOOL
TO CHURCH EDUCATION

*"Go ye therefore, and make disciples of all
the nations, baptizing them into the name of
the Father and of the Son and of the Holy
Spirit: teaching them to observe all things
whatsoever I commanded you: and lo, I am
with you always, even unto the end of the
world."* (Matthew 28:19–20)

A successful and much loved pastor, when asked about the
educational ministry of his church, replied: "The Sunday
school is sick and I frankly don't know what to do about it." In
saying this he was reflecting the despair of many concerned
clergymen and lay people about the educational ministry of the
church. What can we do about the decline in enrollment, the
loss of interest, and the overall ineffectiveness of this aspect of
the church's ministry?

In this chapter I will attempt to analyze the problem and offer in principle a modest proposal for a possible solution. A
good place to begin is to put the teaching ministry of the church
in perspective.

BIBLICAL FOUNDATION FOR CHURCH EDUCATION

The relation of preaching and teaching. Are preaching and
teaching simply two different ways of referring to the ministry
of the Word? In actual practice the institutional church today

has equated preaching with the pulpit ministry, whether it consists of a proclamation of the Gospel, an exposition of a passage of Scripture, an exhortation to obey a Scriptural directive, a topical discourse, or a combination of these things. Teaching, on the other hand, is often thought of as that which takes place outside the pulpit in the classroom or in small groups. According to this view, preaching is of the essence of the church, whereas teaching is something extra.

C. H. Dodd, the celebrated professor of Divinity at Cambridge University, after conducting research in an attempt to determine the content of the primitive preaching of the church, concluded that the New Testament maintains a clear distinction between preaching and teaching. According to Dodd:

> The distinction is preserved alike in Gospels, Acts, Epistles, and Apocalypse, and must be considered characteristic of early Christian usage in general. Teaching (*didaskein*) is in a large majority of cases ethical instruction. Occasionally it seems to include what we should call apologetic, that is, the reasoned commendation of Christianity to persons interested but not yet convinced. Sometimes, especially in the Johannine writings, it includes the exposition of theological doctrine. Preaching, on the other hand, is the public proclamation of Christianity to the non-Christian world.[1]

For Dodd, then, preaching is the message of redemption addressed to unbelievers, whereas teaching is, for the most part, ethical instruction directed to the believer. Preaching and

---

[1]C.H. Dodd, *The Apostolic Preaching and Its Developments* (London: Hodder and Stoughton Ltd., 1944), p. 7.

teaching must be distinguished, from his point of view, because they differ in content and because they differ in the audience to whom the content is addressed.

That there is a distinction between preaching and teaching can be defended on Biblical grounds. The word most commonly translated preaching (*kērussein,* "to herald," used more than sixty times) and the word most commonly translated teaching (*didaskein,* used approximately ninety times) in their root meanings simply do not mean the same thing and are used in different ways. Dodd's rigid distinction, however, and his rationale for it must be challenged.

First of all, one cannot draw a sharp line between preaching and teaching on the basis of dividing Biblical content into *kerygma* (the proclamation of salvation) and *didache* (ethical instruction). The Scripture is a unity. The proclamation of the gospel is never without ethical implications, and ethical instruction is always in the context of God's unfolding plan of redemption. The preaching of the gospel includes elements of teaching, and the wonder of the good news of salvation should always come through in the teaching of the Word of God.

This unbiblical separation of the gospel from ethical instruction serves to reinforce the present tendency on the part of both laymen and clergy to moralize the Scripture; that is, to teach the Scripture as though it contained only a series of do's and don't's unrelated to the person and work of Christ.[2] For instance, instead of Old Testament Bible characters being presented as they are—sinful men and women whom God has chosen and enabled to fulfill His purpose and who need His

<hr>

[2]Cf. also R. J. Rushdoony, *Intellectual Schizophrenia* (Philadelphia: The Presbyterian and Reformed Publishing Co., 1961), pp. 119-122; and James Smart, *The Teaching Ministry of the Church* (Philadelphia: The Westminster Press, 1954), pp. 77-80, 103-107, 146.

grace just as much as we do—they are often pictured only at their heroic best as examples for children to follow. To do this is to ignore the primary purpose of revelation.[3]

The oneness of God's Word is evident in the public ministry of Christ. The kingdom of God was His subject whether He was preaching or teaching. He began His public ministry by preaching, "Repent ye; for the kingdom of heaven is at hand" (Matthew 4:17). He patiently taught His disciples that "the kingdom of heaven is like unto a man that is a merchant seeking goodly pearls: and having found one pearl of great price,

---

[3]This reductionism can be performed in other ways. Consider this not so hypothetical illustration. It is 9:00 A.M. on the Sunday morning before Christmas. The Sunday school lesson for the day is Luke 2:1–7. The teacher has spent very little time in preparation and is almost at the point of desperation. "I don't have enough time to really get into the passage," he says to himself. "Background material and word studies are out. The class could discuss the passage, but there is no obvious practical application here." Then he is struck with a sudden inspiration. He sees in verse seven the handle he is looking for: "There was no room for them in the inn." "How many times," he wonders aloud, "have I heard a sermon on this? All the ways we crowd Christ out of our lives at Christmas time—we could discuss this for hours."

Now, of course, it is true that Christmas is a time when we often get our priorities out of order. But this is not the point. The question is, what does this passage intend to teach? There is no evidence of any malicious intent when the innkeeper turned away Mary and Joseph. He had no control over the fact that there was an enormous crowd in the city which caused all the rooms to be taken. As far as verse seven is concerned, this was simply Luke's way as an historian of explaining how it happened that Christ was born in a cattle trough. Even if the innkeeper had been guilty of objectionable behavior, that still would not justify the teacher's failure to present the ethical principle in the light of the context. Luke 2:1–7 reveals the infinite power and love of God in overruling a pagan leader and the humiliation of Christ in the lowly circumstances of His birth. The cumulative effect of teaching good works apart from the gospel over a period of years is devastating. It produces a kind of religious schizophrenia. With the mind one professes the doctrine of justification by faith, but with the heart he equates Christianity with doing that which is "good" and avoiding that which is "evil." Inevitably there is an inner conflict. It is in such a state as this that the soul cries out: "Wretched man that I am! who shall deliver me out of the body of this death?" (Romans 7:24). In a teaching ministry that is biblically grounded there is not this tension between law and grace. There is, rather, an exposition of the unfolding plan of God in which good works are presented as the fruit of true faith offered up as "spiritual sacrifices, acceptable to God through Jesus Christ" (I Peter 2:5b).

he went and sold all that he had, and bought it'' (Matthew 13:45–46). The Sermon on the Mount (Matthew, chapters 5-7), which is a discourse on ethical conduct, begins ''and he opened his mouth and taught them, saying, Blessed are the poor in spirit: for theirs is the kingdom of heaven. . . .'' (Matthew 5:2ff).

Following the example of Jesus, the early disciples both preached and taught the gospel of the kingdom. Few would deny that Christ was preached (Acts 8:5, 15:21, 20:25). But it should be recognized that the redemptive message of which Christ is the subject was also taught. In Acts 5:42 the Scripture says, ''And every day, in the temple and at home, they ceased not to teach and to preach Jesus as the Christ.'' When Paul was in Rome in the custody of the government he was allowed to live in his own ''hired house'' where he ''received all that went in unto him, preaching the kingdom of God, and teaching the things concerning the Lord Jesus Christ . . .'' (Acts 28:30–31). First century Christians, with a great zeal to serve their Lord and with a passion for souls, used both preaching and teaching to make known the glad tidings of the gospel to all peoples, that they might become disciples of Jesus Christ.

In the second place, Dodd's view that a distinction can be made between preaching and teaching on the grounds that they are directed to different audiences is also subject to question. Preaching in the New Testament was done in the synagogue, in the temple, in private homes, and in open air meetings. Likewise teaching was conducted in all those places. It is only reasonable to assume that then as now the audiences were composed of both believers and unbelievers.

It may be argued that since preaching is by its very nature a proclamation of the good news and a call to decision, it would therefore be applicable only to the unbeliever. Certainly its great importance in evangelism cannot be disputed. The apostle Paul made this abundantly clear when he declared that ''it was God's good pleasure through the foolishness of the preaching to save them that believe" (I Corinthians 1:21b). But is the unbeliever the only one who benefits from the heralding of the gospel? Doesn't the believer need to be reminded of how he was saved, as only one who is fired with the truth of the gospel and impelled to proclaim it can do? What can stir his soul like the preaching of the gospel to the kind of gratitude that constrains him to present himself to God as a living thank offering? And is it not true that the believer, who is also a sinner, needs to be confronted with his need for repentance?

Teaching the Word of God, on the other hand, is thought by some (such as those who agree with Dodd's thesis) to presuppose the conversion of the learner. But this position cannot always be upheld. The Christian parent does not wait until his child is converted before teaching him to pray, read the Bible, and, in short, enter into all that is involved in being a Christian. Moreover, the work of evangelism among people in general is not limited to a simple declaration of the gospel. With the full realization that only the Holy Spirit can give eyes to see and ears to hear "the deep things of God" (I Corinthians 2:10b), the evangelist, in a manner consistent with the divinely ordained laws of human learning, speaks in the language of the hearer and explains each element of the gospel in ways conducive to making it understandable. Although an invitation to receive Christ is an essential aspect of evangelism, many are converted simply through an exposition of the gospel. (Invitation, of course, is implicit in the gospel itself.) Incredible as this may sound to those who remember "religion" classes as those periods right after lunch best spent in sleeping, a colleague recently reported to me that a student was converted as a result of taking a systematic theology course in which the doctrines of grace were taught.

If preaching and teaching cannot be rigidly distinguished on the basis of either their content or their audience, wherein do they differ? In their essential character, preaching and teaching differ as to *form*. Preaching is the proclamation of the Word of God to man as a sinner whether he is an unbeliever or a believer, calling upon him to repent and believe. For the unbeliever it is a call to turn away from sin as the reigning principle of life and to turn unto Christ as Savior and Lord. For the believer it is also a summons to repent of sin, including particular sins, and to stir up the gift of faith which is within him.

Teaching occurs in the context of a personal relationship between teacher and student. It involves imparting knowledge of the Word of God through various means of instruction (exposition, demonstration, illustration, etc.) to man as a learner, whether before or after conversion, with the end in view that the knowledge may be assimilated into his life. When the teaching of the Word is addressed to man prior to conversion it may be a means of evangelism. When addressed to man after conversion it is a means of nurture. The response of the learner is more likely to be gradual than instantaneous. Furthermore, teaching is not a singular event as is preaching. It is a continuous process. One occasion for teaching is related to earlier occasions in such a way that there is an increase of knowledge and a greater depth of understanding. In addition, although there is nothing one can do to guarantee learning at the deepest level, the teacher hopes that such occasions for learning will result in a better assimilation of the truth.

Preaching and teaching are not mutually exclusive. They interpenetrate each other with preaching sometimes dominant (Acts 2:14–39) and at other times with the didactic element prevailing (Matthew, chapters 5-7). But neither are they synonymous. The church has both a preaching and a teaching ministry, and it cannot truly be the church if it neglects either.

The biblical mandate for teaching. In the Old Testament God commanded Aaron to "teach the children of Israel all the statutes which Jehovah hath spoken unto them by Moses"

(Leviticus 10:11). This duty continued to be a priestly responsibility (Deuteronomy 24:8ff., 31:9ff., 33:8ff.). In the New
Testament a basic qualification of the elder is that he be "apt
to teach" (I Timothy 3:2). Paul lists the pastor-teacher as an
office given by Christ to the church for the purpose of equipping the saints for their ministry (Ephesians 4:11–12). In no
passage, however, is the mandate to the church more clearly
stated than in the Great Commission. It is appropriate, therefore, that special consideration be given to Matthew 28:19–20:

> Go ye therefore, and make disciples of all the
> nations, baptizing them into the name of the
> Father and of the Son and of the Holy Spirit:
> teaching them to observe all things whatsoever
> I commanded you . . .

This mandate is clearly addressed to the church. It is important
to observe this because some today, at least in practice, dismiss
the church as an irrelevant hold-over from the past. That the
church is under attack in a hostile world is to be expected.
However, today some of its most serious critics are Christians.

Those on the left accuse the church of being inflexible,
equating the unchanging gospel with an unchanging way of doing things—singing the same hymns in the same way, following
the same order of service, and using the same ritual. This in-
flexibility is one of the objections raised by those pursuing
their religious interests outside the church in the numerous
para-church groups.

At the same time, those on the right charge the church with
following after every theological fad, adhering first to one
theologian and then to another. It was probably with this in
mind that one speaker rather facetiously asked an audience of
clergyman and lay leaders of a particular denomination at its
annual meeting: "Well, who are you reading this year?" Un-

derstandably many seek refuge in groups outside the church which seem more sure of where they are going.

That the church is imperfect and made up of imperfect people, some of whom are guilty of unbelief and hypocrisy, cannot be denied. Reformation *is* needed. But as weak and ineffectual as the church may sometimes appear to be, it is still central to God's redemptive purpose. Gratitude should be expressed for all that has been accomplished through various para-church groups—especially on the college campus, in overseas missions, and in the area of publications. It should be remembered, however, that it is the church with Christ's doctrine, officers, sacraments, and government to whom the commission has been given and the promise made. Any long range solution to real or imaginary problems in the institutional church, therefore, should not be sought in the multiplication of independent organizations, but in an authentic biblical reformation of the church. In this chapter we are especially concerned about the reformation of its teaching ministry.

The mandate to the church is to "make disciples." But what is a disciple? Is it the same as a convert? It is clear from this passage that true discipling involves more than eliciting from someone a profession of faith (although this is included). Making a disciple requires not only the initiatory rite of baptism but also teaching beyond that which precedes baptism. Furthermore, the term disciple means a pupil or apprentice of someone.[4] When applied to a follower of Christ it suggests one who is trained in the way of Christ for service in His kingdom.

Making a disciple, it must also be pointed out, goes beyond making a pupil. In today's academic setting the pupil may be drawn to the teacher because of what the teacher knows, the

---

[4]Gerhard Kittel, ed., *Theological Dictionary of the New Testament,* Vol. IV (Grand Rapids: Wm. B. Eerdmans Publishing Co., 1967), p. 416.

cause he represents, or perhaps the credentials he is able to provide. The pupil is somewhat detached from the teacher and may agree, disagree, or reserve judgment on whatever is presented to him. The disciple of Christ, on the other hand, is drawn to Him for what He is in Himself-Savior and Lord. The whole of the disciple's life—his thinking, feeling, willing—is shaped by the Lord.[5] Paul's very moving testimony, "For to me to live is Christ . . ." (Philippians 1:21a), is in effect a beautiful description of this unique relationship between Christ and His disciple.

The means by which the church is to make disciples are twofold. First of all, there is the initiatory rite of baptism which signifies admission into the fellowship of the church. In the case of adults, conversion is prerequisite to baptism. Secondly, disciples are made by teaching those admitted into the fellowship of the church. The ministry of the Word that God is pleased to use in converting sinners prior to baptism is not all that is required. Much more ("all things whatsoever I have commanded you") needs to be taught and taught in such a way that the initiated are prompted to practice ("observe") it in every area of life. There is no indication here that a disciple receives a specified amount of training over a certain period of time at which point his training is complete and he is then prepared to serve. Whether "whatsoever things I have commanded you" is limited to the Gospel account or extended to the whole of God's Word, the scope of the content and the requisite ability to apply it to all situations necessitates continuous training. Since the essence of the disciple's training is his observing what Christ commanded, continuous service is also required. The disciple, therefore, never ceases to be a learner in the school of Christ or a servant in His kingdom.

[5]*Ibid.*, pp. 441ff.

The vitality of the church may be measured by its response to Christ's command to "make disciples." The Book of Acts, which is a selective history of the early church from c.30-60 A.D., is a thrilling account of the expansion of the church through the making of disciples "in Jerusalem, and in all Judea and Samaria," and beyond Palestine to Asia Minor and Europe. Through much of the next three centuries many converts were thoroughly instructed in the faith before and after baptism as the church continued its spiritual conquest across the Graeco-Roman world. Although some of this period was marked by controversy and compromise, the growth of the church, nevertheless, was so spectacular that church historian Philip Schaff was prompted to remark: ". . . about the end of the third century the name of Christ was known, revered, and persecuted in every province and every city of the empire."[6] To be sure, the root cause of the success of the early church was spiritual rather than methodological, but indisputably the former produced the latter.

The Middle Ages were the low point for the church. The masses had few educational opportunities. Ignorance and indolence abounded in the church. The clergy were not equipped to teach the laity, and thus the laity were not equipped to teach their children. Ritualism was substituted for the preaching and teaching of the gospel. On almost every front the church appeared to be impotent. But, as always, God had not left Himself without a witness. Some Christian instruction was given through the monastic orders. And during the latter part of this period a number of small groups operating from both within and without the Church of Rome continued to preach and teach the Word of God. From these groups there eventually

<hr>

[6]Philip Schaff, *History of the Christian Church* Vol. II (Grand Rapids: Wm. B. Eerdmans Publishing Co., 1970), p. 22.

came men like John Wyclif and John Hus who were among the forerunners of the Reformation.

Ironically, a revival of learning in which scholars found their intellectual delight in pagan literature was indirectly a factor that led to the Reformation, which in turn gave a new direction and a new impetus to learning for centuries to come. Reformers such as Luther, Melanchthon, Calvin, Zwingli, and Knox looked upon education as a natural outcome of their faith and an essential means for implementing their theological, ecclesiastical, and civil reforms. There has never been a time in church history when the church, family, school, and state were so closely tied together in promoting Christian education.

By the end of the eighteenth century, however, the religious fires lit during the Reformation began to burn low. The church had left its first love again. Rationalism was having its day even in the church. Paradoxically the spiritual decline in the church was paralleled by a great revival which spread through England, America, and Europe. As Kenneth Scott Latourette, the well-known church historian, observed: "From one angle, never had the prospect for Christianity seemed so grim. From another, never had the faith been so widely spread or exerted such extensive effects on mankind."[7] It was in this kind of setting that the Sunday school began to emerge as the primary means for Christian education.

[7]Kenneth Scott Latourette, *A History of Christianity* (New York: Harper and Brothers, 1953), p. 1055.

THE SUNDAY SCHOOL:[8] AN INSTITUTION
THAT HAS NEVER FOUND A HOME

For more than a century the Sunday school has been the chief educational agency of the Protestant Church. It has at times provided basic education for the poor; it has been an effective vehicle for evangelizing the unsaved; and for countless thousands it has been the only means for receiving Bible training. At the same time, it has become a synonym for theological shallowness; it has often been charged with moralism as to the way the Scripture is taught; and it has not produced a high degree of Biblical literacy. These factors are important in that they reflect, at least to some degree, the failure of the Sunday school to bring to bear the Word of God upon the total lifestyle of the person. When viewed in the light of the biblical mandate to teach converts "to observe all things whatsoever I commanded . . ." the Sunday school does not measure up very well. Something must be done. But what? Should we try to improve the Sunday school by upgrading and updating it? Should we abandon it in favor of something else? Or is there another way? Before a solution can be proposed, there is still a prior question that must be answered, namely, why doesn't the Sunday school measure up? It is axiomatic that a remedy cannot be prescribed until the cause of the illness has been determined.

How the Sunday school came to take up residence in the church. One of the most significant causes of the problem as described above is that the Sunday school has never been in-

---

[8]Cf. H. Clay Trumbull, *Yale Lectures on the Sunday School* (Philadelphia: John D. Wattles, 1888). A classic on the origin and methods of the Sunday school. He believed that "the Sunday-school . . . represents God's chosen agency, from of old, for the evangelizing and for the instruction of those whom his Church is set to reach and to rear . . ." (p. vi).

tegrated with the total ministry of the church. The Sunday school began outside the church and in a sense has remained that way until this day.

The first Sunday school was organized in 1780 by Robert Raikes in Gloucester, England. It met in a private home. The purpose of the school was "to check the deplorable profanation of the Sabbath"[9] by poor children who, released from employment on that day, spent their time "in noise and riot, playing at 'chuck,' and cursing and swearing. . . ."[10] The courses of instruction included reading and writing as well as the study of Scripture, which apparently was used primarily as the basis for moral training. The Sunday school was not organized in the interest of making disciples (as this term has been previously defined). It did, however, meet a real need. Raikes, the proprietor and publisher of the *Gloucester Journal*, used his newspaper to publicize the Sunday school. Through this means the idea spread rapidly throughout England even in the face of strong opposition from the established church.

The Sunday school as developed by Raikes was ideally suited to the cause of the evangelical revival of the late eighteenth century. Some method was needed for carrying on a work among children and for the training of converts lest the effect of the revival be of short duration. Evangelical leaders such as John Wesley, recognizing the importance of the Sunday school for their purposes, were able to use it to conserve the fruit of the religious awakening and to accelerate the growth of the revival movement. This use of the institution had a formative and lasting influence on the Sunday school. By the end of the eigh-

[9]Ellwood P. Cubberly, *Readings in the History of Education* (Boston: Houghton Mifflin Company, 1920), p. 514.
[10]*Ibid.*

teenth century the essential character of the Sunday school as an institution, existing apart from the church, being operated by laymen, and serving as an instrument for evangelizing children, had already been formed.

In America the earliest Sunday schools were based on the Raikes model, but after a short period of time a significant change took place. There was no continuing need here for a separate school for destitute children. Therefore, after the first quarter of the nineteenth century, the Sunday school was limited almost exclusively in its approach to moral and spiritual training. In this capacity it became the primary agency for pioneer evangelism. The story of the American Sunday School Union, a nondenominational society which dominated the Sunday school movement from 1824 to the 1860s, is a thrilling account of selfless laymen reaching others for Christ through the planting of Sunday schools. It is indeed noteworthy that in a large proportion of these schools the work resulted in the establishment of churches. But there is another side of the story that must be told.

As an independent institution, the Sunday school understandably had its own worship service, its own curriculum, and its own means of support. Not so understandable is that this continued to be true even after the church began to enlist the Sunday school to teach the sectarian elements that had been removed from the public school. What we have today is in effect an institution within an institution. The Sunday school is housed in the building of a particular church, but it is not to any great extent integrated with that church's total ministry.

Consider the following illustration which is admittedly drawn a little larger than life in order to dramatize the problem. In the home of the typical church family who attend the First Presbyterian Church of Midville, Sunday morning is often a rather hectic time as parents try to get themselves and their children ready to go to "Sunday school and church."

Sunday school begins about 9:45 A.M. (this means anytime between 9:45 A.M. and 10:00 A.M.) with an assembly period (a separate worship service) which includes an opening prayer, hymns, and the recognition of all who have had a birthday during the past week. The leader also reads the appropriate Scripture reading from the Uniform Lesson Series, a curriculum material that is designed to relate the Sunday school to other Sunday schools on an interdenominational basis, rather than to the ministry of the local church with which it is associated. At 10:00 A.M. everyone goes to his appropriate class for a thirty to forty minute session. Each class begins with the calling of the roll (a separate roll is kept for the Sunday school) followed by the taking of an offering (a separate offering is taken for the support of the Sunday school). As the teacher begins the lesson the attention of the class is divided between the teacher's words and the jingling of coins and rustling of paper by the secretary-treasurer, who is sitting near the rear of the room counting the offering and getting all the reports in order. This bookkeeping has to be completed as soon as possible because a short time after the class begins the Sunday school superintendent (a separate administrator for this part of the educational ministry of the church) comes to get the offering and roll book. (All Sunday school business must be done during the time allotted for the Sunday school.) Finally, just as time is running out at the end of the session, the teacher asks, "Now how many of you are going to stay for church?"

Why is it that after more than a century of association with the institutional church, the Sunday school is still viewed and administered as though it were a separate institution? The root cause, of course, is spiritual in nature. But one of the most obvious secondary causes is what Francis Schaeffer has called "ossified conservatism";[11] that is, the mindless and thought-

---

[11]Francis Schaeffer, *The Church at the End of the 20th Century* (Downers Grove, Illinois: Inter-Varsity Press, 1970), p. 76.

less way that many modern churchmen have of carrying on the work of the church.

A story of unknown origin that has enjoyed general circulation through the years helps to illustrate this point. A young housewife was busy in the kitchen preparing a ham for the evening meal. A neighbor who happened to be visiting just at this time noticed that she cut off a third of the ham before putting it in the pan. Thinking this to be somewhat out of the ordinary, she asked her hostess the reason for this unusual procedure. The young housewife pondered the question for a few moments but was unable to give a satisfactory reply. "You know," she said, "I really don't know. My mother did it this way. It was she who taught me how to bake a ham, and so I've just always done it this way." The incident set the young housewife to wondering why it was that her mother prepared a ham for baking in this particular way. So the next time she saw her mother she couldn't wait to talk to her about it. "Mother," she asked, "why do you always cut off a third of the ham before baking it?" Her mother, a little taken aback by the question, thought about it for a moment and then replied, "You know, I really don't know. My mother did it this way, she always baked marvelous hams, and it just never occurred to me to do it any other way." By this time the young housewife's curiosity had been aroused. As soon as possible she paid a visit to her grandmother and asked her the same question. With a twinkle in her eye, the older lady said, "Well, honey, there is no real mystery about it. When your mother was a little girl we were so poor that we couldn't afford a pan large enough to contain a whole ham. So I had to cut off enough of the ham to make it fit in the pan."

Is it possible that this type of thinking has been characteristic of the twentieth century church? This mindless way of approaching human tasks results partly from our living in an age in which people have been conditioned to ask "how," but only very rarely to ask "why." The whole concept of the Sunday school is a holdover from its previous existence as a para-church agency. At that time the church had lost its zeal for ministering to children, leaving a void for some such institution as the Sunday school to fill. When the church was compelled by circumstances to take up the kind of religious training that was being set aside by the public school, the church had the opportunity to develop a plan for a full-orbed educational ministry consistent with its own nature and mission. It was decided instead to adopt the Sunday school almost intact.

Why is this so important? What difference does it make that the Sunday school has never been integrated with the total ministry of the church? The answer is revealed in a consideration of some of the major problems that have grown out of this situation.

Some problems related to the lack of organizational integration. First of all, there is the obvious separation between clergy and laity. Inasmuch as the Sunday school traditionally has been regarded as being of, by, and for the lay people, ministers as a rule have adopted a hands-off policy. As Robert Lynn and Elliott Wright observed: "Most ministers remain indifferent to Sunday school affairs unless some unusual trouble arises."[12] Indeed, very little of the minister's time is spent on the educational work of the church. This writer has had the experience of conducting weekend workshops for Sunday school teachers and administrators in which the minister of one or more participating churches made only a token appearance or did not attend at all.

The lack of a meaningful association between the minister and the Sunday school is one of the most important reasons

[12]Robert W. Lynn and Elliott Wright, *The Big Little School* (New York: Harper and Row, 1971), pp. 96-97.

why the lay teacher is not adequately trained. If, for example, all the professional teachers in the schools, kindergarten through the university, suddenly withdrew from their work as educators, the overall level of education would be greatly reduced in a relatively short time. This is in fact what has actually happened in the church. The pastor-teacher has withdrawn from his mandated task of equipping lay teachers for their ministry. An occasional workshop conducted by imported professionals is helpful as supplementary training. Nevertheless, it is hardly a substitute for the continuing involvement of a well-prepared pastor-teacher[13] with the lay teachers whom he has been called to serve, in an atmosphere of mutual respect and love built up over a long period of time.

The indifference of the minister to the educational ministry of the church, which he tends to equate with the Sunday school, is also reflected in his use of the pulpit. Sermon after sermon is preached on evangelism, missions, and various aspects of stewardship, and rightly so. But seldom is heard a word of encouragement or exhortation on the subject of the educational ministry of the church. It is very difficult for even the most highly motivated lay people to carry on and strengthen the church's educational ministry with little or no support from the church's pulpit.

Secondly, the lack of organizational integration has resulted in a curriculum design that is based upon the nature and mission of the Sunday school as defined by tradition, rather than the nature and mission of the church as interpreted by the creeds of the church. Evangelicals have historically regarded

---

[13]The seminarian who identifies the Sunday school as that which is run by lay people and equates the Sunday school with the educational ministry of the church is often not very highly motivated to pursue seriously courses of study in the area of professional church education. This is a problem that departments of Christian education in theological seminaries have to overcome.

the Sunday school as an instrument for evangelizing children and as a means for teaching the first principles of the faith. A curriculum designed to meet only those objectives does not go far enough. It provides "milk" for "babes" but not "solid food" for "fullgrown men" (Hebrews 5:13–14). Moreover, since the Sunday school is thought of as separate from the church, there is not the same expectation for curriculum materials to conform to the creeds of the church as there is for the sermon to do so. The Sunday school being basically interdenominational, the unwritten standard applied to curriculum materials is that of the teachings of evangelical Christianity as a whole. Surely it is very confusing for a church member to hear Reformed doctrine taught from the pulpit and evangelical arminianism taught in the classroom.

Liberal churchmen, embarrassed by the lay-operated Sunday school with its homespun theology, attempted at first to do away with it, but soon found out that they were overmatched by their more conservative grass-roots opponents. J. C. Wynn candidly recalls: "I had my own comeuppance some twenty years ago in writing an article for *The Christian Century* in which I tolled the bell for a decent burial and kind obituary for the Sunday church school. My article never laid a glove on the institution. . . ."[14] Forced to accept the fact that the Sunday school was likely to be around for sometime to come, the liberal establishment determined to make it more compatible with their own views. Taking their cue from such organizations as the Religious Education Association and the International Council of Religious Education (today the Division of Christian Education of the National Council of Churches), they were partially successful in introducing into the Sunday school

[14]J. C. Wynn, *Christian Education for Liberation* (Nashville: Abingdon, 1977), p. 14.

many of the ideas of secular educators such as John Dewey. For much of the first half of the twentieth century the educational theory and practice used in the Sunday school, although overlaid with theological views from right to left according to its constituency, was in large measure borrowed from public education.

Some contemporary approaches to the problems of the Sunday school. The institutional church as a whole is of one mind in recognizing that there are serious problems related to the Sunday school. But there is little unanimity either in the analysis of the problem or in the solution offered. Understandably the variety of approaches taken today reflects the diversity of theological viewpoints and cultural backgrounds within the church.

Generally speaking, evangelicals apparently see nothing wrong with the Sunday school that improved materials and methods can't correct. What is needed, according to this outlook, are curriculum materials that are more up-to-date, colorful, and appealing to those outside the church, as well as to those who regularly attend Sunday school. They are also concerned with the development of teacher aid materials and in the promotion of workshops for the training of teachers in the latest methods of teaching and the most effective ways of motivating people. While these measures may be very helpful, their value is more that of a temporary palliative than it is a long range cure, because they address the symptoms of the malady rather than its root causes.[15]

[15]There are, of course, many evangelicals who take a much more creative approach. Lawrence O. Richards, perhaps the most prolific evangelical writer in the area of church education, is an outstanding example. In his *A Theology of Christian Education* (Grand Rapids: Zondervan, 1975), he rightly warns us: "Isolating the 'educational ministry of the church' from the congregation's total life is a deadly error" (p. 24). He argues eloquently for a wholistic ministry by the whole body of believers to the whole person. Using his understanding of ecclesiology rather than a more theocentric perspective as his starting point, however, he is inevitably pushed to the development of an educational model that overemphasizes the context of the teaching and learning process at the expense of the content.

Neo-orthodox church educators who have become entrenched in some of the main line denominations quite correctly see the problem as the failure to relate what one believes about God, man, revelation, truth, and the church to the way one views educational theory and practice. Following up on this line of thought they have developed curriculum materials such as the *Faith and Life* series of the Presbyterian Church, U.S.A., along with appropriate teaching strategies which have been designed to implement their philosophy of church education. This action represented a radical departure from the earlier practice by both conservatives and liberals of uncritically using anything current in secular educational methodology as long as the content was theologically acceptable. The difficulty with this approach was that in the remote areas those who manned the teaching and administrative posts in the Sunday school found the new materials and methods very difficult to use. Those in the main line denominations self-consciously committed to evangelical Christianity were attracted to the emphases of neo-orthodox educators on family nurture and the necessity of relating educational theory and practice to theology. At the same time, however, these people found their theological stance to be irreconcilable to that of the neo-orthodox educators on such matters as the acceptance of higher criticism and the separation of revelation from the Scripture.

Although neo-liberalism with its constantly changing face has no program to reform the Sunday school, it is worthy of mention here, as it bears a definite influence on the content of curriculum materials of main line denominations. Every self-respecting church curriculum planner, so it is thought, must be current. Robert Lynn and Elliott Wright explain it this way:

> Publication of Harvey Cox's *The Secular City*
> signaled a new interest in "worldly" theology.

No sooner had this perspective been incorporated into the curriculum of the mainline denominations than the needle of fashions swung unsteadily toward "death of God," "hope," "black theology" and "joy of celebration." Sunday school literature planners and writers entered the 1970s as weary victims of a one-year cultural lag. Hoping to be current, the best they could do, given publication schedules, was to keep up with what was the rage the year before.[16]

This situation would be humorous if it did not have such tragic implications.

Indeed, there is obviously still a real need for an even greater effort among evangelical and Reformed people in this area of ministry. How can we develop in the church an educational approach consistent with our theology? In the continual process of working out an answer to this question and applying it in the life of the church, an ongoing dialogue among those of like faith would be of invaluable help to all concerned. The remainder of this chapter is part of the contribution this writer would make to such a discussion.

CHURCH EDUCATION:
A PLAN FOR MAKING DISCIPLES

At various times over the past century and a half the church has added the Sunday school, the Sunday evening youth fellowship, the vacation Bible school, weekday Bible studies, and discipling programs, and the list goes on and on. In each case

---

[16]Lynn and Wright, *op. cit.*, p. 92.

the activity or program was simply added without reference to the existing program and without consideration as to how it would fit into the total picture. There is too much at stake to allow this practice to continue. The time has come for responsible church leaders—both clergy and laity—to sit down together and ask themselves some serious questions. What is the mission of the church? What is the most efficient and consistently Biblical means of carrying out this mission? How can existing programs be changed or strengthened to meet the above objective?

More important than the right form is the right spirit. Form and spirit do not always go together, but the former may be an outward indication of the latter. To allow the various programs of the church to develop without any overall design or purpose is to indicate a lack of unity between the clergy and laity and to show the failure of God's people as a whole to love God with all their minds as well as with all their hearts.

Starting with the situation as it is now, educational reform begins as do other reforms in the church—in the hearts and minds of those whom God has moved to dream dreams of what ought to be, and who cannot rest until the vision becomes a reality.

A shared vision. Without a vision the people become locked into a mindless, lethargic routine. On the other hand, the thought of a local particular church in which the members are discipling others even as they are being discipled; in which the whole counsel of God (Acts 20:27) is applied to the whole of life and addressed to the whole person in a context of Christian love; in which all that is done by the teacher outside or inside the classroom complements all that is done in the pulpit, in the service of worship, in the evangelistic outreach, and in the ministry of compassion, is enough to excite even those who already know what it means to be excited about the things of God, and to move them to action.

It is imperative that the senior pastor-teacher have this kind of vision. Aside from spiritual qualifications there is no quality of leadership more important than the ability to visualize what ought to be done and then cause others to share that vision. The necessity of the pastor's involvement cannot be stressed too much. No matter how much the team ministry idea is emphasized, the pastor is still the most visible and influential leader in the church. Wherever there is a good pastor-parishioner relationship, there is a high degree of correlation between the pastor's emphases and the congregation's emphases. The churches that are well-known for their contributions to foreign missions, for example, almost always have a pastor with a burden for this cause.

Much tradition has to be overcome, however, in order for the pastor and the layman to be united in those things that concern the educational ministry of the church. Likewise much needs to be overcome in bridging the gulf between the professional church educator employed by denominational boards and the local church teachers and administrators. Lynn and Wright contend that this separation is related to the inevitable struggle between the expert and the volunteer in American society. According to their analysis of the problem

> specialists and common men find it nearly impossible to agree on goals and methods. The church intellectual urgently trying to reach and bring up the mass of people to his level of comprehension is often so isolated from those he seeks to touch that most of his efforts bring disappointing results.[17]

Although the seminary is in a strategic position to serve as a

[17]*Ibid.*

catalyst for educational reform, in reality it mirrors the lack of integration in the church. Until those of us involved with the training of men for the ministry get our own house in order, we will continue to be, as far as church education is concerned, more a part of the problem than the solution. The current interest in curriculum revision in the established seminaries and the willingness of many church leaders today to innovate in theological education are encouraging signs.

One matter is certain. There can be no educational reform that does not include both clergy and laity. All the grandiose designs for church education in the world will be to no avail if the grass-roots of the church are not convinced of their validity and are not willing to give their support. The idea for reform may begin with either the pastor or the layman, but it must be a shared vision lest it be merely an exercise in idle dreaming.

A shared strategy. A shared vision to which God's people are sincerely committed calls for a shared strategy by which the church may begin to make the vision a reality. This strategy should include: (1) a statement of objectives, and (2) a curriculum design.

A statement of objectives. Objectives have obvious functional values such as providing direction, economizing effort, and supplying a basis for evaluation. A value of objectives that is often overlooked is their use as a means of integration. Starting with the mission of the church as the overall objective, the governing body of the local church can develop significant subordinate objectives that tie each aspect of the church's ministry to this overall objective and to each other. With respect to the educational ministry of the church the following statement of objectives is suggested:

1. That each person understand and be committed to the whole counsel of God.
2. That each person understand and be committed to the right use of the Word, the sacraments, and prayer.

3. That each person understand and be committed to Jesus Christ as his Lord and Savior.
4. That each person understand and be committed to the system of doctrine taught in the Scripture.
5. That each person understand and be committed to right participation in the life of the church of Jesus Christ.
6. That each person understand and be committed to the task of of making disciples of every nation.
7. That each person understand and be committed to living under the Lordship of Christ in the whole of life.

The above educational objectives are based on the writer's understanding of a biblical view of the learning process. Those who define learning as behavior modification believe that all objectives should be stated in behavioral terms. For example, they would substitute phrases such as "to be able to identify" or "to be able to recite" for the phrase "to understand." The problem here is that "to be able to identify" or "to be able to recite" is not the equivalent of "to understand." The understanding of some area of truth cannot be reduced to one or more behavioral components, although the former may result in the latter. Only when performance is the objective should objectives be stated in behavioral terms, such as to be able to write legibly, to be able to speak clearly.

A curriculum design.[18] The content of the curriculum grows out of the educational objectives. Thus, if a local church were planning a curriculum based on the objectives suggested previously, the content would include: an extensive (survey) and intensive (individual books) study of the whole Bible as God's unfolding plan of redemption for His people; a study of the

[18]For another perspective on the curriculum within the Reformed tradition, see A. H. DeGraaff, *The Educational Ministry of the Church* (Delft, Judels, and Brinkman, 1966), especially chapter IV.

church, its history, its creeds, its worship, its mission, and its government; and a study of the Christian life—what it means to be the people of God. If this seems to be somewhat similar to the curriculum of a theological seminary, it is not by accident. Prospective clergymen should not have exclusive access to this type of preparation. And if the church is serious about all of its members using their particular gifts in carrying out the mission of the church, then they need this kind of training for the same reasons the minister needs it. Of course, to equip adequately the saints for their ministry involves more than engaging them in formal study. In the training of a believer for discipleship, opportunities for practice must be provided as well as opportunities for classroom instruction. A danger to be avoided, however, is overreacting to what we perceive as a one-sided emphasis in church education, and simply going to the opposite extreme. A goal for which to strive is a God-centered approach in which all of these emphases mutually complement each other in a total program of Christian education.

The curriculum design of the church, unlike any other educational agency, should cover the whole span of life—from infancy to old age. Regrettably the twentieth century church has bought a humanistic idea that age is bad and youth is good. "We've had our day," say many older adults. "Let's do something for the young people." The point here is not that age is good and youth is bad, but that every age group is important and has its own opportunities and responsibilities. The Scriptures teach that "though our outward man is decaying, yet our inward man is renewed day by day" (II Corinthians 4:16b). For the believer, therefore, Browning's words are true, "the best is yet to be."[19] This being the case, the curriculum plan-

---

[19]Robert Browning, "Rabbi Ben Ezra," in *The Literature of England: An Anthology and A History*, Vol. II, ed. by George B. Woods, Homer A. Watt, and George K. Anderson, 3rd ed. (Chicago: Scott, Foresman, and Company, 1948), p. 698.

ners should provide just as many exciting opportunities for study and learning for older adults as they do for any other age group.

The other end of the age scale is also frequently neglected. Not even the most die-hard classicist would argue for a formally structured curriculum for infants. At the same time it should be recognized that a child is never too young to learn. In planning for infants, curriculum designers should give great attention to the quality of nonverbal teaching—for example, the way the child is handled and the warmth of the physical environment. It is also particularly important that the nursery teacher, as well as the young or prospective parent, be trained in the implications of the covenant for the nurture of children.

Finally, the courses of study should be distributed throughout the week according to an overall plan. Some classes would be conducted on Sunday morning, others on Sunday evening, and still others on a weekday afternoon or evening. This is very much like the present format as far as the time of meeting is concerned. The difference is that it would involve one unified curriculum. With each course of study designed to implement in a coordinated way the educational objectives adopted by the local church, the various educational ministries of the church would be interrelated. Instead of Sunday school, youth fellowship, discipling programs, and leadership training, there would be *church education,* and, at the same time, the curriculum would be integrated with the total ministry of the church.

A shared task. While church education is the responsibility of the church as a whole, the specific function of teaching in a formal sense is shared by the pastor-teacher and those lay people with the gifts and calling to teach.

The pastor-teacher. Pastors and teachers comprise one class of those officers listed in Ephesians 4:11 given to equip believers for their individual ministries in building up the church.

In this passage "pastors and teachers" are understood to mean two functions of one office, hence the use of the hyphenated title pastor-teacher. Obviously the title itself suggests that one of the most important ways in which the pastor-teacher equips the saints is through teaching. There are many occasions on which this may be done. Let me point out two such occasions that are especially relevant to the teaching ministry of the church.

First of all, the pastor-teacher's most significant formal opportunity for teaching is in the pulpit. It should be remembered that the worship service is much more than an occasion for instruction. Even so, to the extent that the pastor-teacher teaches in the pulpit he should be cognizant of the educational objectives adopted by the local church and guided by biblical principles of pedagogy. Generally speaking, the pastor-teacher has failed to do this, with the tragic result that many church-goers are ignorant of the content of their faith, even after years of regular church attendance. J. Stanley Glen comments:

> In the practical planning of the pulpit program, the selection of sermons is usually at random from any part of the Bible, except for the occasional series. The resulting fragmentation of the wholeness of the biblical books and passages adds its own measure of confusion. . . . It is not difficult, therefore, to understand why so many otherwise gifted and capable Christians grasp so little of the intelligible content of the faith they profess, even after hearing hundreds of sermons over the years. It derives from the fact that the task of homiletics is so largely divorced from Christian education.[20]

[20]J. Stanley Glen, *The Recovery of the Teaching Ministry* (Philadelphia: The Westminster Press, 1960), pp. 13-14.

What a difference it would make if doctrinal terms were explained and illustrated with due regard to the background and circumstances of the congregation. How helpful it would be if a sermon was used to introduce the biblical theme that was to be the subject of study in the classroom. What an aid it could be to understanding the message if occasionally when the sermon dealt with an especially difficult or provocative topic, a question-and-answer session based on the content of the message could be conducted with the congregation during lunch after the service or at the next midweek service.

Recently I preached in a small church in a neighboring town. My text for the sermon was John 14:1–6 which deals with the subject of life after death. This is indeed a topic in which many are interested, especially older people. After the service I had lunch with one of the church families. No sooner had we sat down to eat than they began asking questions about the sermon, seeking either additional information or clarification of points that were unclear. No teacher could have asked for a better opportunity for teaching. If this kind of teaching could occur with one particular family, why not with the church family as a whole?

Secondly, the pastor-teacher should teach those who teach others (Ephesians 4:11–12; II Timothy 2:2). This involves both a structured and an unstructured approach. If the lay teacher is to be brought to the high level of knowledge and skill needed for teaching in today's world, he must have advanced formal instruction. Certainly there is no more exciting or useful way for the pastor-teacher to spend his time than in getting together with a group of lay teachers and exploring in depth those areas of study that would be most useful to them in carrying out their task.[21] The instruction that was begun in a formal setting

---

[21]See appendix for bibliography of teacher training materials.

119

should be carried over into an informal one-to-one relationship. In this context questions can be answered in a way that is relevant to the particular situation, resources can be suggested to fit specific problems, attention can be focused on areas which need improvement, and encouragement can be given as it is needed. This practice should continue until there is evidence that the truth first presented in the classroom has been assimilated into the trainee's life. This kind of training is discipleship carried to the utmost degree.

Is this not expecting entirely too much from the pastor-teacher? How can he take on the awesome responsibility of training teachers when he is already overloaded? A partial answer to this question would call for the minister to reexamine his priorities and reorder his schedule. He can say "no" to some of the invitations he receives to speak in other churches, youth conferences, and civic clubs; he can turn down some of the opportunities he has to attend seminars and workshops around the country; he can even turn over some of the administrative details of his church to others. But he cannot under any circumstance abdicate his responsibility to equip the lay teachers of his church for their ministry. If the pastor-teacher is too busy to do this, he is indeed too busy.

If a church becomes so large that the task of teacher training cannot be performed directly by the pastor-teacher, it would be wise for the church to consider employing a minister of Christian education (ordained) or a director of Christian education (unordained). The M.C.E. or the D.C.E. is an extension of the role of the pastor-teacher. In a sense the M.C.E. serves *in loco pastoris* (in the place of the pastor). This is not to imply that he usurps the prerogatives and responsibilities of the pastor-teacher but rather that in close connection with him he carries on a teaching ministry that would otherwise not be possible.

120

The lay teacher. The Scripture declares: "according as each hath received a gift, ministering it among yourselves, as good stewards of the manifold grace of God. . ." (I Peter 4:10). From this passage it can be seen that every Christian has a ministry for which he is accountable to God. On this point there is no difference between clergy and laity. Thus when the layman is confronted with the opportunity to serve in the church, the question for him is not whether he has a ministry but rather whether this particular form of ministry is the one to which God is calling him and for which He will hold him accountable.

This attitude runs directly counter to the practice of voluntarism, a habit deeply ingrained in American church life and devastating in its effects. By voluntarism I mean the notion that ministry is optional for the layman. If a layman rejects an opportunity for service in the church, all concerned react with indifference or, at most, disappointment. On the other hand, if he accepts an invitation for ministry he is looked upon as having granted the church a favor. One occasion when this attitude is most conspicuous is when recruiting a lay person for teaching in the church.

Consider the following illustration in which the recruiter approaches the prospective lay teacher:

> Mrs. Brown, we need a teacher for the junior high department. All of us on the committee have just racked our brains and we can't seem to come up with anybody who would be willing to take on this responsibility. We thought that since all of your children are grown and no longer in the home you might be willing to consider it. It wouldn't take much of your time. You wouldn't have to spend as much time in preparation for junior high's as you would an older class. Won't you please at least think about it? We just have to find somebody and

you would be doing us such a favor if you
would agree to do it.

Now even if Mrs. Brown responds favorably to this plaintive
plea for help, she is likely to give only the irreducible minimum
for which she has been asked. If she misses a class without telling anyone or if she fails to make adequate preparation,
nothing too much is thought about it either by her or by the
church officials who administer the educational program.
After all, what more could be expected of a volunteer who
serves at her leisure?

Think of the difference it would make if the recruiter used a
Scriptural approach with the prospective lay teacher. Imagine
the following request:

Mrs. Brown, there is a need in the church for a
committed Christian with the gift of teaching
to teach a junior high class. This is one of the
most challenging opportunities for ministry in
the church. Dealing with young people at this
stage of their lives is indeed an awesome responsibility. They need someone who will be
well prepared in class, who will take the time to
get to know them as individuals outside of
class, and who will continue to grow as a Christian teacher by availing himself of the leadership training opportunities provided by the
church. After much prayer and thought we believe that God is leading us to confront you
with this opportunity for ministry. We don't
want you to give us an answer until you have
had time to consider prayerfully and thoughtfully whether or not this is a ministry to which
God is calling you. If you should then come to
concur with us that this is God's will for you,

please know that we would support you in your ministry, not only with our prayers but also by providing whatever training or counsel you may need.

Isn't this coming on too strong? Won't people be turned off by this approach? What is often overlooked is that even on a purely psychological basis no one really wants to do a job that is unimportant and that requires little of him. More important, however, is that this approach is more consistent with the high calling of God for every Christian. The church cannot take lightly that which God esteems highly.

As the church moves into the last decades of the twentieth century it needs to reexamine in the light of Scripture not only its nature and mission, but also the means by which this mission is to be accomplished. Our Lord was quite clear when He said to a small band of disicples, "Go ye therefore, and make disciples of all the nations" (Matthew 28:19a). He was equally clear when He set forth teaching as a means by which this was to be done. If this is true, church education must be a high priority on the agenda of the institutional church as a whole, of every church court, and of every thoughtful Christian.

6

THE CHRISTIAN TEACHER

"Whatsoever ye do, work heartily, as unto the Lord, and not unto men; knowing that from the Lord ye shall receive the recompense of the inheritance: ye serve the Lord Christ." (Colossians 3:23–24)

Teaching is bringing to the student direction, stimulation, encouragement, and the interpretation and application of the truth. In short, teaching brings all that is needed for the student to learn the truth. We must go on to say, however, that teaching may occur without learning. We could go even further and say that teaching at its very best does not guarantee learning. To say otherwise would be to negate the responsibility of the learner,[1] a fact so often overlooked today. Yet we must also say that authentic teaching has as its end the assimilation of the truth into the student's life and the use of that truth in the service of Christ. Teaching is never simply a bare presentation of the facts with no thought to what happens afterwards in the life of the student.

Thus defined, teaching is an integral part of the learning process and demands that we give serious attention to the role of the one who engages in this activity.

[1]See chapter two, especially pp.   –

THE IMPORTANCE OF THE ROLE OF THE TEACHER

Teaching is a divinely ordained means by which God advances His kingdom (Matt. 28:20; 2 Tim. 2:2; Deut. 6:7). It is therefore a high and holy calling. This is true whether we are talking about a professor in a theological seminary, a pastor-teacher in his church, an unordained teacher in the school or church, or a parent in the home.

Sadly enough, the general public today does not share this high view of the role of the teacher, especially the elementary and secondary school teacher.[2] Sadder still, many teachers do not share this high view of their role. It has been my observation that when a teacher is asked by a layman what he does for a living, he often looks around to be sure no one else is listening and then answers, "I am just a teacher." It is as though the teacher feels that he is doing something that is not quite up to what the world expects of a successful person. On the other hand, if a member of a well paid and highly respected profession is asked the same question, he is likely to look around to be sure he has everyone's attention before proudly announcing the nature of his work. If the foregoing observation is correct, it is not just a commentary on the value system of a materialistic society, it is even more a disclosure of the woeful ignorance of the teacher as to the importance of his calling. If he had any understanding at all of the high place of teaching in the plan of God for the gathering and perfecting of the saints and for the advancement of Christ's kingdom, he would draw

---

[2]As a teacher I have in weaker moments winced and in better moments laughed when I have heard such familiar put-downs as: "If you can do something, do it; if not, teach; and if you can't teach, teach education." This is due, at least in part, to the general public's tendency to lump all professional educationists together. This, of course, makes no more sense than lumping all theologians together, or all philosophers.

himself up to his full height and gratefully declare to anyone who wanted to know, "I AM A TEACHER. THANK GOD! I AM A TEACHER."

The anti-intellectualism spawned by some of the current secular philosophies of education[3] is at least partly responsible for the low esteem in which teachers are held. There is a direct corollary, for example, between one's view of the nature of truth and one's view of the role of the teacher. If truth is relative, as some contemporary educators believe, then the teacher does not have to become knowledgeable of subject matter, for there is no body of truth to be known; he does not have to become proficient in the art of communicating truth, for there is no truth to be communicated; he does not even have to make a clear distinction between his role as a teacher and that of the student, because there is no truth which could serve as the basis for making such a distinction.

Believing that God is the Author of all truth and that He has ordained teaching as a means of communicating His truth, the Christian educator may have a high and holy view of his vocation. A Christian may be called to serve in positions which are more in the public eye than teaching, or in places which are more distant and exotic than in a classroom with twenty-five wiggly children, but he can never be called to serve in a position of greater usefulness or in a place that is more strategic. Humanly speaking, what formal education means to the child will depend more upon the teacher than any other factor. The administration of the school, therefore, must give the highest priority to the kind of faculty it brings to the students.

[3]See chapter seven, especially pp. 147-161.

THE THREEFOLD FUNCTION OF THE TEACHER

Christ executes the offices of a prophet, priest, and king as our Redeemer.[4] In Christ all believers have a priestly, prophetic, and kingly function to fulfill as His servants.[5] In the following section my purpose is to relate those functions to the work of the Christian teacher.

The kingly function. The kingly function involves the exercise of authority. The teacher makes assignments, sets standards for academic achievement, establishes and enforces boundaries for acceptable behavior, and generally lays down the ground rules by which all the various school activities are to operate. In a word, the teacher rules over his class. If someone objects that the practice of one person ruling over another is dehumanizing, we may answer that this is true only if the teacher wrongly uses his authority. Such cases as the classroom teacher who is quick to use "put-downs" such as "you can't ever do anything right no matter how many times I tell you how to do it," or the high school band director who frequently has temper tantrums and throws his baton at a student who displeases him, readily come to mind as examples of the abuse of authority. Admittedly, this is not the kind of school environment that is conducive to the development of a healthy self-image.

But authority may be used in another way. The Christian educator rules under the authority of One greater than himself, even Jesus Christ. Under this kind of rule the pupil is nurtured in an atmosphere of love; he is accorded the respect due one

---

[4]The Westminster Shorter Catechism, Q.23.

[5]John Calvin, *Institutes of the Christian Religion,* Vol. 1, Book II, Chapter 15 (Grand Rapids: Wm. B. Eerdmans Publishing Company), pp. 426, 427, and 431. See also a discussion of this topic by Cyril Eastwood, *The Priesthood of All Believers* (Minneapolis: Augsburg Publishing House), pp. 66-69.

who is made in the likeness of God; he is liberated from the mass confusion that frequently prevails in the modern classroom; and he is pointed to One greater than the teacher as the One to whom he owes his ultimate obedience.

For the humanistic educator, the question is not whether authority should be used arbitrarily, but rather whether it should be used at all. In his book *Emile* (1762), Rousseau set forth his naturalistic philosophy of education. Here he described a character who grew up in a flower garden. No external restraints were imposed on him. He was given no information for which he did not ask. Rather, he was permitted to grow naturally to become all that he had the capacity to become as his teacher removed obstacles which were beyond his competence to handle and remained in the background to provide help whenever Emile called for it. The character and the experiment, however, were products of Rousseau's imagination.

Nevertheless, this idea has permeated "progressive" education. It is abroad today, especially in our great metropolitan areas. The principle that no external restraints should be imposed on the student is based on the assumption that the child is basically good, and if left alone will develop naturally into that which is perfect. This idea is responsible for much of the widespread rebellion against parental authority, ecclesiastical authority, and civil authority—but rebellion most of all against God.

The Christian believes that the child is sinful and that if he goes on his natural way his end will be not perfection, but perdition—not knowledge, but ignorance—not wisdom, but folly. There must be a radical change in the child's life and then he must be nurtured in the way of the Lord. Authority must be exercised. It must be exercised in love and in keeping with the maturity of the child, but it must be done. The teacher dare not abdicate this responsibility.

The prophetic function. A prophet is one who speaks for God. Ascribing a prophetic function to the classroom teacher of a subject matter other than theology presupposes that all truth—mathematics, history, science, and language, for example—is God's truth. This is not to infer that there is no distinction to be made between the Holy Scripture and the arts and sciences. The Scripture alone is the infallible authority for faith and life. It does mean, however, that truth cannot be divided into sacred and secular categories. If all truth comes from God, then all truth is sacred. And whosoever communicates the truth under the direction of its Author is indeed a spokesman for God.

An additional comment should be made concerning the normative use of Scripture in Christian education. While we do not go to the Scripture for the overall content and method of the various disciplines found in the school curriculum, the Scripture is the only place we can go to discover the origin, meaning, and purpose of any aspect of reality. The integration of faith and learning is therefore the basic task of the Christian educator.

Such an integration is certainly a laudable goal, but how do we achieve it? After all, integration is a very complex matter involving all facets of the educational program, i.e. the curriculum, and instructional methodology. Even the design of a building reflects the philosophy of an institution. Obviously the place to begin is with the recruitment of teachers who are spiritually mature. In those classrooms in which the teacher is so steeped in the Scripture that his heart and mind are shaped by revealed truth, there are daily unplanned occasions in which the integration of the Christian faith and learning takes place. When questions are raised in class involving basic values, the teacher will have at least the basis for an answer. When a problem arises in a relationship with a student or a colleague, the teacher's response of necessity will be affected by his daily walk with the Lord. Without such an authentic embodiment of the truth of Christ and the love of Christ in the teacher's life, all planned attempts to integrate faith and learning will be artificial and contrived.

According to Frank Gaebelein, the esteemed founder and long-time headmaster of the Stony Brook School, integration is greatly facilitated if the teacher of so-called secular subjects is also used as a teacher of the Bible. He contends:

> The Christian school that believes all truth to be God's truth and that is serious about making Christ and the Bible integral to its curriculum must give up the concept of a completely separate Bible department. Instead it must seek and develop devoted Christian teachers who, along with competency in mathematics, science, languages, or social studies, are also able to give instruction in Bible.[6]

I believe this principle has its most relevant application at the elementary school level at a time when the child's developmental needs are best served by an able subject matter generalist in a self-contained classroom.[7]

---

[6]Frank E. Gaebelein, *The Pattern of God's Truth* (Chicago: Moody Press, 1968), pp. 48-49.

[7]Gaebelein applies this principle to the secondary school level. In all deference to one of the foremost pioneers in Christian education, I have some reservations about the secondary school giving up a separate Bible department. At this level it is necessary to have a Bible specialist who is as competent to explore Biblical studies with his students as his colleagues are in their subject matter specialty. The system should not be so structured as to suggest to the student that there should not be the same type of in-depth study of the Scripture as there is in the area of mathematics or literature or history.

Some years ago when I was beginning my first year as the headmaster of a Christian elementary school (K-6), we made use of the director of Christian education, who served on the staff of the church with which the school was associated, to teach Bible in the lower elementary grades. In each grade the regular teacher in the self-contained class was allowed to use the Bible class time as her free period while the D.C.E. conducted the class. Administratively this arrangement seemed to be a very sound procedure. The Bible was taught by a very knowledgeable instructor and the regular teacher had some much needed time for planning, grading, or just to catch her breath. What we had failed to realize, however, was that the elementary age child, who has not yet been culturally conditioned to separate the sacred from the secular, is not at all inhibited in relating what was presented in Bible class to any other activity during the day, whether it be in the selection of a topic for a creative writing assignment,or in the making of a value judgment in a class discussion. The next year we asked the regular classroom teacher to teach the Bible, and other provisions were made for her free period. This change helped the teacher immeasurably in becoming more proficient in the handling of God's Word and at the same time put her in a much better position to assist the student as he made intellectual trips back and forth between the Bible and the other areas of the curriculum.

Finally, the teacher must self-consciously interpret each subject matter area in the light of a biblical view of the origin, nature and purpose of reality. On this point the objection is often raised: "but isn't mathematics, history, and language arts the same for everyone?" One has only to do a cursory survey of current school textbooks to find the answer. A world history book based on an evolutionary view of history, a biology text written on the assumption that man is simply a more complex form of animal life, and a basal reader making no distinction in the function of male and female in society, are all cases in point. Inevitably the author of each textbook interprets the material according to his own non-demonstrable faith principles.

What a difference it makes when the Christian teacher brings his own faith perspective to bear on the subject he is teaching. Consider, for example, a Christian view of language arts. The Christian teacher understands that language is a gift of God and that He has made man accountable for its right use. Moreover, the Christian teacher believes language to be the divinely ordained means for communicating the truth about reality. This means that words are to be filled with meaning;[8] that communication is to be personal, clear, and truthful—not only in content but also in form and style; and that every tongue, whatever the mode of expression—oral or written, poetry or prose—be used in a way that makes most for the glory of God.

Only the Christian has a world-and-life view which can provide a unifying principle for the curriculum as a whole. It is the Christian teacher's task, therefore, to apply his world view in imaginative and creative ways in the classroom so that the student is challenged to think through the implications of his faith for every aspect of life. The whole truth for the whole person for the whole of life under the Lordship of Christ is an appropriate battle cry for the Christian educator in his ongoing struggle with the forces of secularism.

[8]The price of goods and services is not the only thing that is inflated today. Words are more and more becoming so extended in their usage that they actually mean very little. For example, when a word like curriculum is used to mean everything that a child experiences in the school, its meaning not only becomes unintelligible, but we are also forced to find some other expression to communicate the original meaning of the word. This is one of the reasons why we find ourselves using more and more words to say less and less.

The priestly function. The priestly function involves a number of responsibilities, but only a few will be mentioned here. First of all, the teacher is responsible to embody before the pupil the truth which he is seeking to communicate. This means that he must have an authentic faith for which he is willing to live and to die.

Spiritual maturity is the most essential qualification to be considered in the selection of a teacher either for the educational program of the church or for the Christian school. Strangely enough it has been the church more than the Christian school that has not taken this qualification seriously in the recruiting of teachers. The church has all too often followed the notion that if an irregular and irresponsible church member is given a job such as teaching a Sunday school class, then this may help him to become a more regular and more responsible member. It does not work that way. Ordinarily an undependable church member makes an undependable teacher. The church member in question is not helped and the students are left without a qualified teacher.

The Apostle Paul stressed the importance of experience in the faith on the part of those who would be church officers. He warned that the elder should be "not a novice, lest being puffed up he fall into the condemnation of the devil" (1 Tim. 3:6). Turning to the office of the deacon he cautioned: "And let these also first be proved; then let them serve as deacons, if they be blameless" (1 Tim. 3:10). The principle that Paul set forth here is clear. Only those who have already demonstrated spiritual maturity should seek an office in the church. The principle may be extended to apply to other areas of ministry. Certainly the very nature of the work of teaching requires that this principle be applied to the Christian teacher. If the pupil does not learn the truth from what the teacher is, he is not likely to learn it from what he says.

Secondly, the Christian teacher makes his work an offering

to God (Col. 3:23–24). He does not work primarily for pay, although a laborer is worthy of his hire; he does not work primarily for the applause of men, although the honest appreciation of others is something for which he can be sincerely grateful; and he does not work primarily for personal satisfaction, although being fulfilled in one's vocation is one of God's greatest blessings. Rather, he performs his task for One greater than self, even Jesus Christ, and discovers that all other needs are provided for him.

Thirdly, the Christian teacher offers up prayer to God on behalf of his students. A revered seminary professor once shared with some of us who sat under his ministry his own experience with intercessory prayer. He said that when he was in the pastorate he would go over to his study at the church very early on Sunday morning, take out the church roll, get down on his knees and earnestly pray for each member by name. Hearing about his experience made a lasting impression on my life. What greater work could he have done for his people as he prepared for the morning worship service.

It occurred to me that intercessory prayer is also an integral part of the ministry of the teacher. Picture the classroom teacher early in the morning beginning the day in the presence of God by holding up his students to the throne of grace, praying for them by name, laying before the Lord their specific needs. James wrote: "The effectual fervent prayer of a righteous man availeth much." Without this kind of prayer very little that is truly worthwhile can be accomplished, but with it only God knows the great and marvelous things that can be done.

THE QUALIFICATIONS OF THE TEACHER

Christian education at all levels and in every educational institution requires the use of teachers who are authentically

Christian. This requirement cannot be stressed too much. Nevertheless, there are many very mature Christians who are not qualified to teach. What then are some of the basic qualifications that peculiarly qualify a person to be a teacher?

The gift of teaching.[9] There is a sense in which all Christians have the gift of teaching. The Christian parent is enabled to obey the command to bring up his children "in the nurture and admonition of the Lord" (Eph. 6:4b, KJV). The typical Christian young person is able to share with a friend in a reasonably clear and understandable way what a passage of Scripture means to him. But when the Scripture refers to teaching as a distinctive gift (Rom. 12:7, 1 Cor. 12:28, and Eph. 4:11) with the clear implication that it is possessed by some and not by others, it has in view an unusual and identifiable ability to understand the truth, conceptualize it in terms common to a large range of people, and explain it to them.

But how does the Christian's gift of teaching differ from the non-Christian's ability to teach? Certainly all must recognize that there are many non-Christians who have exceptional ability to communicate ideas to other people. To be sure, the difference is not one of intellect or of teaching skill. It is rather in the natural man's inability to truly understand the things of God (1 Cor. 2:6–14). The natural man, as was pointed out in chapter two,[10] knows the truth only in a relative sense. For instance, he can know that water may be used to put out a fire and he can act on that information, but he cannot understand the ultimate origin, nature, and purpose of this aspect of reality. While there may be great value in the content of the non-

---

[9]This is not to imply that a Christian has only one gift. He may have several. It all depends on the good pleasure of God.

[10]See chapter two, p. 32.

Christian's instruction, if his teaching is taken uncritically it can only lead to a distorted view of the world and to the further development of a man-centered culture.

Some may feel that the gift of teaching is related only to the teaching of the Bible. This is understandable. After all, the Holy Scripture is the inspired Word of God. It sits in judgment upon both our reason and experience. It directs and corrects the Christian's understanding of every area of life, including the various subjects which make up the curriculum. The Bible is indeed of singular importance.

Yet, the Scripture's centrality in no way diminishes the fact that all truth—the truth of physics as well as the truth of Scripture—comes from God. If this fact is so, then no aspect of truth can be rightly taught except by those who have been given the grace to interpret and explain it from the perspective of God's Word.

How does a person know whether or not he has the gift of teaching? Is it possible for a person to spend his whole life searching for his gifts and never find them? The answer is that the gift of teaching as well as all other gifts for ministry can be discovered. God does not play games with us. If a servant of Christ wants to find out whether or not he has the gift of teaching, there are some very practical things he can do. First of all, he can earnestly and regularly pray for God's guidance. There is no substitute for this. Secondly, he can respond to opportunities for teaching, especially within the Christian community. For example, he can take a turn at teaching a Sunday school class or at leading a home Bible study. There may even be an opportunity to teach an occasional class in the Christian day school. Even though a person may not be trained to teach at the time of his initial efforts, if he has potential as a teacher it will very likely be demonstrated. The evident blessings of God on one's teaching in the lives of others and the positive evaluation of competent Christian observers (Gal. 2:9) are significant indications that one in fact possesses the gift of teaching.

This gift is precious. How greatly it is used in the service of Christ! The possession of such a marvelous gift should be the cause for great thanksgiving, but never the grounds for vain boasting. In 1 Corinthians 4:7 the Scripture says:

> For who maketh thee to differ? And what hast thou that thou didst not receive? But if thou didst receive it, why dost thou glory as if thou hadst not received it?

Paul put things in their proper perspective. The gift is to be prized because it comes from God. But the recipient of the gift is not to indulge himself in vain glory, because he has done nothing to deserve it. The reading of this passage is especially recommended to the teacher whenever he feels an "attack of ego" coming on. This writer ought to know. I have often been compelled to come back to these words of the apostle for correction and reproof.

A call to teach. Consider the following exchange between a minister and an elder in his church. "Why are you a preacher?" the older man asked the new pastor in town as he was visiting in the parishioner's home for the first time. The young pastor, just beginning his first work, was quick to respond, "Sir, I am a preacher because God has called me to preach the Gospel." Now this pastor's reply is consistent with the general agreement among evangelical Christians that if a man is not convinced of his call to preach, he has no business in the pulpit. I concur with that judgment.

But what about those vocations for which ordination by a church is not required? Are not fields of labor such as law, medicine, agriculture, and education also divine callings? I believe that they are. The calling to belong to Jesus Christ (Rom. 1:6) encompasses all that one is and all that one does. Thus all lawful human labor may be a divine calling. Carl Henry put it this way:

> The layman has a calling in Christ no less than the minister. . . . Life's variety of callings implies no distinction in the respective value or dignity of those engaged therein; God's purpose in the calling is the discriminating factor and not man's superiority or inferiority. God is served by obedience, not by self-chosen vocations (cf. Isa. 1:11–17; Hos. 6:6; Matt. 9:13; 12:7); no gift, whether mental or physical, is genuinely *devoted* to society except in and through the "call." Faithful obedience to God's call makes the clergy as good as, but no better than the devout merchant or shoemaker.[11]

Of course, the same could be said for the teacher, whether he is a professional or a layman. When the teacher is asked the question, "Why are you a teacher?" it is equally important that he be able to reply, "because God has called me to teach His truth."

The call to a particular ministry can be determined. Reflecting on the way in which God dealt with men such as Peter and Paul, one would conclude that He works with each person as an individual in terms of his unique personality and circumstances. The testimony of many Christian friends through the years has confirmed this. There are some very definite steps, however, that every Christian should follow in determining

---

[11]Carl F. H. Henry, *Aspects of Christian Social Ethics* (Grand Rapids: Wm. B. Eerdmans Publishing Company, 1964), pp. 43-44.

whatever it is he has been called to do. He should assess his own gifts, he should be especially sensitive to the burden or burdens that God has laid on his heart, and he should evaluate on biblical grounds his motives for wanting or not wanting to do a specific work.

Through it all, the born-again believer can claim a very special promise. In the book of Proverbs it is written:

> Trust in the Lord with all thine heart; and lean not unto thine own understanding. In all the ways acknowledge Him, and He shall direct thy paths (Prov. 3:5–6, KJV).

The conditions of this promise are two-fold: first of all, a wholehearted confidence in God; and secondly, the recognition of God in every public and private undertaking. When one has done this God will give him the spiritual discernment he needs to make the right decision.

A love for the student. The book of 1 Corinthians was written by the Apostle Paul to the church at Corinth in response to information which he had received concerning a number of problems within the church. One of these problems had to do with the attitude of the Corinthian Christians towards the use of spiritual gifts. For instance, there were some who glorified in having certain gifts and looked down upon those who did not possess them. Apparently for these people the gifts had become an end in themselves. They had no real interest in using their gifts for the benefit of others. In chapters 12-14 Paul addressed this particular concern. He explained that all gifts come from the same Spirit who sovereignly distributes them according to His will (1 Cor. 12:4–11). The implication was that if the one Spirit gives various gifts to accomplish His purpose, then obviously it was not His intention that the possessors of these gifts be in competition with each other.

Paul illustrates this by likening the church to a body. Each member of the body is essential and has its own special value (1 Cor. 12:12–19). The Apostle goes on to describe the folly of one member of the body denying the importance of a less conspicuous member (1 Cor. 12:20–21) and the wisdom of every member caring for each other according to his need (1 Cor. 12:24–25). Continuing this train of thought, Paul encouraged the Corinthian Christians to seek the best gifts, not necessarily the ones most honored among men but those which edify others and build up the body of Christ (1 Cor. 12:27–31a).

Suddenly the Apostle interrupts his discussion of spiritual gifts in order to call to the Corinthians' attention "a more excellent way," without which even the best gifts are worthless. Paul put it in these words:

> If I speak with the tongues of men and of angels, but have not love, I am become sounding brass, or a clanging cymbal. And if I have the gift of prophecy, and know all mysteries and all knowledge; and if I have all faith, so as to remove mountains, but have not love, I am nothing. And if I bestow all my goods to feed the poor, and if I give my body to be burned, but have not love, it profiteth me nothing (1 Cor. 13:1–3).

The application for the teacher is clear. If one has the gift of teaching so that he could explain all the mysteries of the universe, and yet has not love, he is nothing and his teaching is mechanical and fruitless.

Love is the fruit of the Spirit (Gal. 5:22). Anyone—believer or unbeliever—may have personal affection for others, but only the believer has the kind of love described in 1 Corinthians 13. Love compels the teacher to rejoice over the students' successes and weep over their failures; to pray for them by name according to their needs; to know them as persons; in short, to give himself in order to help his students realize the potential which God has given them. Without love nothing worthwhile can be done, but with love only God knows the great and mighty things that may be accomplished.

An interest in teaching. Many people are able to exercise enough self-discipline to do well on their job even if they do not particularly like what they are doing. It is very difficult, however—perhaps even impossible—for one to do the work of a teacher successfully if he does not enjoy the task itself.

The nature of teaching itself requires a joy in its execution. One cannot, for example, do such things as develop a sensitivity to the special needs of students or stimulate their thinking with provocative ideas if his heart is not in what he is doing, no matter how hard he may try.

There is also a psychological reason to be considered. When the teacher's task is exciting to him, his teaching is more likely to evoke a positive response from the student. Augustine, one of the greatest of the church fathers, in speaking of teaching, said, "Indeed, people listen to us with much greater pleasure when we ourselves take pleasure in this same work of instruction."[12] Knowledge of content and teaching strategy are important, "but our chief concern, " he declared, "is what means we should adopt to ensure that the catechizer enjoys his work; for the more he is able to do so, the more agreeable will he prove."[13] The converse of this statement is also true. The teacher who has no joy in teaching tends to set up psycholog-

[12]Augustine, *The First Catechetical Instruction,* translated by the Rev. Joseph P. Christopher (New York: Newman Press, 1946), p. 17.
[13]*Ibid.*

ical barriers between the curriculum and the student and between himself and the student.

An interest in teaching is a characteristic that has been common to all teachers who have had fruitful ministries. William Lyon Phelps, the celebrated Yale educator, described his love for teaching in this way:

> I do not know that I could make entirely clear to an outsider the pleasure I have in teaching. I had rather earn my living by teaching than in any other way. To my mind, teaching is not merely a life work, a profession, an occupation or struggle: it is a passion. I love to teach. I love to teach as a painter loves to paint, as a musician loves to play, as a singer loves to sing, as a strong man rejoices to run a race.[14]

Every truly competent teacher can empathize at least to some degree with these feelings. He can only imagine what a farmer feels when he looks over the fields he has planted and sees the crops growing; what a doctor feels when the health of the patient begins to improve and he knows he has been used in the saving of a life; what an artist feels when he stands back and looks at a freshly-completed canvas; what a businessman feels when he has concluded a business transaction that benefits the client as well as himself. But because he is a teacher, he knows the joy a teacher feels when he sees in the face of a pupil the recognition of some truth which has dawned on him for the first time and realizes that for that child, life can never be the same again.

---

[14]As quoted in an article entitled "Teaching as a Man's Job" in *Phi Delta Kappa,* prepared by a committee of Phi Delta Kappa, E. A. Lee, chairman (Homewood, IL, 1958), p. 56.

The preparation of the teacher. Unlike the above characteristics, there are some essential qualifications for teaching which are acquired through training and experience. These include:

An understanding of a Christian world-and-life view and its application to educational theory and practice. There is a difference between being an educator who is also a Christian and in being a Christian educator. The Christian teacher must be equipped to bring his faith perspective to bear upon every aspect of his task as an educator. In this connection publishers such as Baker, Inter-Varsity, Presbyterian and Reformed, and Zondervan—to name only a few—offer helpful resources to both the professional and the lay teacher.

An in-depth knowledge of the subject. There is a tendency, especially by the lay teacher, to prepare just enough to meet the demands of the next class. This, of course, makes for a very superficial learning experience. The professional teacher must spend his life mastering the subject matter area he teaches. The lay teacher involved in the educational ministry of the church must also be a diligent student. In this regard the church has an obligation to provide its teachers with advanced training (training beyond that which is received in the Sunday school) in Bible, doctrine, church history, evangelism, and missions.

An understanding of the divinely ordained laws of child growth. Sadly enough, evangelical Christian scholars have done very little work in the area of developmental psychology. Secular studies such as those done by Piaget or the Gesell Institute are helpful, but they must be viewed critically; for instance, an adolescent rebelling against his parents may be consistent with the statistical norm for human behavior, but it falls woefully short of the biblical standard. As a result of experience the teacher becomes generally knowledgeable about the behavioral characteristics of the age group for which he has a special responsibility. But, in the final analysis, the teacher comes to truly understand the individual student only as he develops an authentic personal relationship with him.

An understanding of the teaching-learning process. What is the nature of learning? How does the pupil learn? What is the optimum environment for learning? These are some of the questions with which the Christian teacher has to wrestle. Here again evangelical Christian scholarship has not offered much help in the field of educational psychology. What then is a Christian educator to do? The answer is that he can develop a Christian world-and-life view. In so doing he will no longer be at the mercy of the secular educator. Instead, he will be able to profit from their work without being taken in by the implications of their non-biblical presuppositions. The Christian teacher can also begin to work through some of the problems on his own or in association with other Christian educators.

Proficiency in the use of instructional methods. If a person has the gift of teaching, knows his subject, and loves the student, he will find a way to impart the truth to him. The Christian teacher, however, cannot stop at that point. He is obligated as a servant of Christ to find the best possible ways by which he can communciate His truth.

Lecture, discussion, question and answer, story-telling, and role-playing are commonly used instructional methods. They can be rationally described and empirically acquired. Teachers can improve their proficiency in the use of these techniques through such means as study, observation, practice, and self-evaluation. Although these methods may be learned, "(they) can become dynamic," as Bavinck says, "only in the living expression of a personality."[15] For the Christian, therefore, the redeemed personality itself is the primary method of teaching.

[15]Cornelius Jaarsma, *The Educational Philosophy of Herman Bavinck* (Grand Rapids: Wm. B. Eerdmans Publishing Company, 1935), p. 165.

Each teacher has something unique to give. He need not copy anyone else. The Christian teacher must always work to sharpen his skills but he must never forget his identity in Christ.

Method is not an end in itself. Busy work has no place in the Christian's teaching strategy. Neither is it a means for helping one cope with a changing world in which there are no absolutes. Rather, for the Christian, method is a means to the end of communicating the truth of God.

No matter how qualified the human teacher may be, he cannot do his work apart from the Divine Teacher. As Dr. J. B. Green has said, "The Spirit's office as Revealer of new truth is finished. . . . But the Spirit's work as Witness and Interpreter is permanent. It is needed by each succeeding generation."[16] It is the Holy Spirit Who illumines our minds, gives us an understanding of the Scripture (John 16:13), and enables us to apply this understanding to every aspect of reality. Let the Christian teacher and student, therefore, approach their respective tasks in humble reliance upon the Divine Teacher, without whom nothing can be known truly.

These first six chapters have been an attempt to set forth a Christian view of education as an alternative to the humanistic views that are so deeply entrenched in the world today. In the last chapter these views will be critically evaluated.

[16] J. B. Green, *Studies in the Holy Spirit* (New York: Fleming H. Revell, 1936), p. 55.

A CRITIQUE OF CONTEMPORARY PHILOSOPHIES OF EDUCATION

"Where is the wise? where is the scribe? where is the disputer of this world? hath not God made foolish the wisdom of the world?" (1 Cor. 1:20)

For much of the twentieth century the Christian community has relied heavily upon the educational theories and practices of secular education. For example, the experience-centered curriculum of the church school, as illustrated by the graded curricula in many of the main line denominations in the 1950s, was similar in principle to the experience-centered curriculum then advocated for the secular school. The same could be said about teaching methods, discipline, classroom management, and evaluation procedures.

Unhappily, much that has been classified as "Christian education" has often been little more than a thin veneer of theology covering a man-centered view of education. To some extent this has been true of Christian educators all across the theological spectrum.

In a large measure we have only ourselves to blame. We have allowed ourselves to be deceived into believing that education is somehow philosophically and religiously neutral. This is, of course, impossible. The ultimate end of education, the nature of the persons educated, and the nature of truth are religious questions. The answers to these questions may be either Christian or non-Christian, but in every case they will be religious answers. They cannot be neutral.

Let me call your attention to three non-Christian philosophies or world views that continue to exert a very formative influence upon both general and church education.

JOHN DEWEY AND PRAGMATISM

"In this century in America," Marcus J. Priester has pointed out, "the philosophic tradition that has been most influential in education is that form of empirical and experimental philosophy characterized by the term 'pragmatism.' "[1] The evidence seems to more than justify this conclusion.

First, most of the professional literature in the field of education is written from a pragmatic point of view. Moreover, schools of education frequently reflect a decided bias for the writings of such well-known pragmatists as John Dewey, William H. Kilpatrick, William James, Boyd H. Bode, John Lawrence Childs, and Theodore Brameld. Perhaps one of the clearest indications of the influence of this philosophy is that the lay person often identifies professional education with this view.

Although pragmatism is a modern twentieth-century philosophy, its roots go back to antiquity. One finds in this school of thought seeds sown by Heraclitus and the Sophists as well as more recent scholars such as Francis Bacon, Auguste Comte, Charles Sanders Pierce, and William James. However, it remained for John Dewey to bring together the various ideas and shape them into a comprehensive system of thought.

[1]Marcus J. Priester, "Philosophical Foundations for Christian Education," in *An Introduction to Christian Education,* ed. by Marvin J. Taylor (Nashville: Abingdon Press, 1966). p. 64.

Dewey taught at Columbia University from 1905-1930. During this time he achieved world-wide recognition as a leading authority in education. Many of his students became prominent teachers in schools of education throughout the United States. His books—*Democracy and Education,* for example—are still regarded as classics in the field.

What then are some of the beliefs of contemporary pragmatism? When one gives a brief treatment of another's beliefs, especially the beliefs of someone with whom he very much disagrees, there is always the danger of oversimplifying, or presenting a distorted picture. Recognizing this as a problem, I will make a conscientious effort to set forth some of the basic assumptions of this school of thought as accurately and fairly as possible.

First of all, for the pragamatist the only reality for man is his own experience. This is a key concept and is related to everything else the pragmatist believes. Let me illustrate.

As a Christian, the first thing I want to know when talking to a person of another religion is what he believes about God. Since the pragmatist believes there can be nothing beyond his own experience—that is, no transempirical reality—he rejects the supernatural.

It is not enough, according to Dewey, simply to maintain an agnostic position with reference to the supernatural. True, in the interest of intellectual integrity one must acknowledge that one does not know what he does not know. "But," Dewey maintains, "generalized agnosticism is only a halfway elimination of the supernatural. Its meaning departs when the intellectual outlook is directed wholly to the natural world."[2]

If indeed there is no reality beyond man's constantly chang-

---

[2]John Dewey, *A Common Faith* (New Haven: Yale University Press, 1934), p. 86.

ing experience, then there is no room in one's thinking for an immutable God "with whom is no variableness, neither shadow of turning" (James 1:17, KJV), or for a Christ who is "the same yesterday, and today, and forever" (Heb. 13:8).

Wayne Rood, who writes very sympathetically about John Dewey, reports that "when . . . Dewey published *A Common Faith* in the mid-thirties, a reviewer in *The Christian Century* welcomed him into the Christian faith. In the next issue in the 'Letters to the Editor' section was a letter from Dewey acknowledging the review but declining the welcome."[3]

Dewey, with his empirical frame of reference, believed that the scientific method, not divine revelation, was the final arbiter of all questions of fact. In the application of this method to the question of transempirical reality, he was just as much opposed to the liberals as he was to the conservatives in the Christian community. He realized that if one admits the existence of the supernatural, evangelical Christianity has a reasonable case. In the continuing controversy in the church, the conservative, although completely opposed to Dewey's basic presuppositions, would find much comfort in these words:

> The modern liberal version of the intellectual content of Christianity seems to the modern mind to be more rational than some of the earlier doctrines that have been reacted against. Such is not the case in fact. The theological philosophers of the Middle Ages had no greater difficulty in giving rational form to all the doctrines of the Roman church than has the liberal theologian of today in for-

[3]Wayne Rood, *Understanding Christian Education* (Nashville: Abingdon Press, 1970), p. 134.

mulating and justifying intellectually the doctrines he entertains. This statement is as applicable to the doctrine of continuing miracles,
penance, indulgences, saints and angels, etc.,
as to the trinity, incarnation, atonement, and
the sacraments. The fundamental question, I
repeat, is not of this and that article of intellectual belief but of intellectual habit, method
and criterion.[4]

Pragmatism is the philosophy that has put so much emphasis on the whole man. Yet it deals with man as though he
doesn't have a soul, as though he isn't made in the image of
God. Man is believed to be a dynamic, behaving organism that
is part of nature and is continuous with it. He is the product of
a long and continuous process of evolution.

Beginning with a man-centered view of reality, the
pragamatist has no difficulty in accepting a naturalistic, evolutionary view of the origin of things. Although all men are different, as each aspect of nature is unique (hence the pragmatist's emphasis on individual differences in education),
there is nothing about man—his intellect, his emotions, his
will—that is not of the same piece as the remainder of nature.
Man is an individuated aspect of nature. He has no spiritual dimension. The "whole man," whom the pragmatist has repeat-
edly emphasized in educational literature, has no soul. He is
simply a behaving organism interacting with other behaving
organisms.

Consider then the implications of the pragmatist view of
reality. Man is shut up in a world of his own experience, inter-

[4]John Dewey, *A Common Faith,* pp. 33-34.

acting with other human beings in a constantly changing environment. That is reality. For him, therefore, the goal of life is to enrich his own experience and to do this in such a way as to open up the possibility of further enrichment of his experience. The goal of life is the goal of education. "Education," Dewey said, "Must be conceived as a continuing reconstruction of experience."[5]

When the Christian educator uncritically superimposes his theology on the alien foundation of pragmatism, he tends to emphasize religious experience and de-emphasize the importance of sound doctrine. The question becomes: How can we help the student enrich his religious experience? rather than: How can we equip the student to serve the Lord Jesus Christ? It is to say, in effect, that the chief end of man is to have a satisfying experience.

This is a distortion of Christianity. As a friend recently remarked, "It is more important to be sanctified than to be satisfied." Of course these things are not mutually exclusive. Christ was deeply concerned with the real needs of human beings. But if God is at the center of our thinking, we must primarily be concerned with true religion, and true religion is the only way one can ever find true happiness. Jesus said, "For whosoever would save his life shall lose it: and whosoever shall lose his life for my sake shall find it" (Matt. 16:25).

Another basic principle of the pragmatic view is that the scientific method should be applied to every problem of man. The individual's life is in continuous movement. As long as things run smoothly, everything is fine. Inevitably the flow of ongoing experience encounters an obstacle or a problem. This

[5] John Dewey, "My Pedagogic Creed," in *John Dewey on Education*, ed. by Reginald D. Archambault (New York: The Modern Library, 1964), p. 434.

is a critical time because it presents one with the occasion of making a decision and taking an action which will affect all subsequent experience.

When a person's experience has been interrupted by a problem, if he acts with intelligence he will begin by observing all the facts in the situation that are relevant to the problem. There is a limit to the amount of data he can collect because the problem stems from a felt need in a particular, ever-changing situation. He must act intelligently because experience will not flow smoothly again until the problem is solved.

Observation of the data suggests a solution or a pattern of solutions to the problem. The projected solution or hypothesis is weighed over against other suggested solutions in terms of possible consequences. In the final phase the hypothesis is tested and the results evaluated. The solution is deemed satisfactory if it causes experience to flow smoothly again; thus opening the way for new and expanding experiences.

The knowledge gained in the application of the scientific method to a particular problem may be helpful in meeting similar problems, but it is not to be regarded as absolute truth. Knowledge is tentative and relative and must always be subject to present experience.

More important than the knowledge gained by the use of scientific method is the skill acquired in the use of this method. From this point of view, method is more important than subject matter. As far as the pragmatist is concerned, one of the most important functions a school can perform is to provide the student with the opportunity to have experiences in problem solving. Courses of study should be arranged so as to deal with problems of arithmetic, problems of reading, problems of science, etc.

From the foregoing it is also quite understandable that the pragmatist does not favor a curriculum composed of well-defined subject matter areas arranged in a predetermined sequence. Dewey declares:

> There is . . . no succession of studies in the ideal
> school curriculum. If education is life, all life
> has from the outset, a scientific aspect, an
> aspect of art and culture, and an aspect of com-
> munication. It cannot, therefore, be true that
> the proper studies for one grade are mere
> reading and writing, and that at a later grade,
> reading or literature, or science may be in-
> troduced. The progress is not in the succession
> of studies, but in the development of new at-
> titudes towards, and new interest in, ex-
> perience.[6]

Dealing with a student in terms of his own felt needs is indeed very attractive to anyone genuinely concerned about
people. After some reflection, however, one may begin to ask
himself such questions as: How does a student always know
what is best for him? Does he instinctively feel a need for that
which is good? Isn't it true that there are many real needs we do
not realize until after we have been introduced to some new
area of thought? The Christian, believing that God know better than sinful man, cannot accept the pragmatist's "doctrine
of felt needs."

Finally, the pragmatist is probably best known for his value
system. In a world with no transempirical reality, values are
relative to the experience of the individual. Good and evil must
be determined according to the consequences that result from
each unit of experience. A good act is measured by the results
of the action. Why should one be honest? Because honesty is

[6]*Ibid.*

153

the best policy. If a person is honest, people will think well of him and may reward him.

Some pragmatists would object to such a description, protesting that what they are talking about is what is best for the community, rather than what is best simply for the individual. Nevertheless, further investigation reveals that the pragmatist believes the well-being of the individual to be dependent upon his interaction with other individuals. That is to say, in a sense the well-being of the individual is related to the efficiency of the society of which he is a part. In the final analysis, when the individual is pushed to make a decision on the basis of what is really "real" for him, the question is still: What is best for me?

The first objection that may be raised about this view of ethical values is its starting point. If, as the pragmatist believes, the individual's experience is the test of everything, ethical relativism is defensible. Moral absolutes are inconsistent with a man-centered view of life. On the other hand, if the chief end of man is to glorify God, then it may be reasonably expected that good and evil are determined by the performance or transgression of His will, which evangelicals believe is revealed sufficiently in the Scriptures. This being true, dishonesty is not wrong simply because it results in undesirable consequences but because God has said, "Thou shalt not bear false witness against thy neighbor" (Exod. 20:16). An extra-martial affair is not wrong because of the emotional problems that may result from the affair but because God has said, "Thou shalt not commit adultery" (Exod. 20:14).

Another objection that may be raised against this view of values is that the pragmatist has no way of determining a good or bad consequence. For example, a student with an important examination on Monday wants to know if it would be right for him to stay home and study all day Sunday. He considers the matter in the light of anticipated consequences. If his thinking is more than superficial, he is inevitably confronted with a prior question: What makes a consequence good or bad? If the pragmatist is to answer this question, he must either move to the right and embrace absolutes with which to define good and evil, or move to the left and lay hold of an existential antinomianism, which freely admits that the only thing that really matters is the free, uninhibited choice of the individual.

In summary, the pragmatist has developed an educational theory and practice based upon the assumption that man is a behaving organism for whom his own experience is the only reality and for whom the enrichment and expansion of that experience is the only goal.

B. F. SKINNER AND BEHAVIORISM

B. F. Skinner is a behavioral scientist, but his book *Beyond Freedom and Dignity,* for which he is best known to the general public, is more the work of a philosopher than that of a scientist. In this work he sets forth his views on the nature of man and the basis for making value judgments.

Skinner calls the view that man is "free to deliberate, decide, and act, possibly in original ways," and is "to be given credit for his successes and blamed for his failures," a "prescientific view." Over against this position he posits the "scientific view," which affirms that "a person's behavior is determined by a genetic endowment traceable to the evolutionary history of the species and by the environmental circumstances to which as an individual he has been exposed." Skinner admits that neither view can be proved but insists that "it is the nature of scientific inquiry that the evidence should shift in favor of the second."[7]

---

[7]B. F. Skinner, *Beyond Freedom and Dignity* (Toronto: Bantam Books, 1971), p. 96.

For Skinner, man is not in any unique sense a self-conscious being who defies complete scientific analysis. The self is, in his words, "a repertoire of behavior appropriate to a given set of contingencies."[8] The private inner world of the human being —his thoughts, dreams, and feelings—is of the same nature as the world outside. "The difference is not in the stuff of which the private world is composed," he declares, "but in its accessibility."[9]

Skinner frequently criticizes the use of the term "autonomous man," a concept which he believes threatens the survival of the race. When the Christian theist uses this term, he is referring to the natural man who sees himself as the final arbiter of truth and value. Skinner uses the term "autonomous man" to refer to any concept of man, Christian or non-Christian, which ascribes a measure of freedom or dignity to his life. Thus defined, the idea of an autonomous man is rejected by the behaviorist. For him, the only difference between a pigeon and a man is that a pigeon is a simple form of animal life, whereas the man is a more complex form.

All behavior, whether animal or human, is determined by environmental conditioning. Skinner illustrates this by saying, "The nomad on horseback in Outer Mongolia and the astronaut in outer space are different people, but, as far as we know, if they had been exchanged at birth, they would have taken each other's place."[10] In this same connection he quotes with approval Gilbert Seldes' proposition "that man is a creature of circumstance, that if you changed the environments of thirty little Hottentots and thirty little aristocratic English children, the aristocrats would become Hottentots, for all practical purposes, and the Hottentots little conserv-

[8]*Ibid.*, p. 189.
[9]*Ibid.*, p. 182.
[10]*Ibid.*, pp. 175-176.

atives."[11]

Thus, every aspect of behavior is rooted in an environmental cause. Every response has a stimulus. If one could isolate the stimulus, according to the behaviorist, he could foresee the specific response. By the use of the technology of behavior, the scientist could take a child at birth and program him to become a minister, a businessman, a bartender, or whatever he determined.

What one can do to an animal, he can do to a human being. What one can do to a human being, he can do to the human race. It is with this confidence in the technology of behavior that Skinner advocates the designing and subsequent development of a utopian culture. He proposes a world

> in which people live together without quarreling, maintain themselves by producing the food, shelter, and clothing they need, enjoy themselves and contribute to the enjoyment of others in art, music, literature, and games, consume only a reasonable part of the resources of the world and add as little as possible to its pollution, bear no more children than can be raised decently, continue to explore the world around them and discover better ways of dealing with it, and come to know themselves accurately and, therefore, manage themselves effectively.[12]

All of this quite obviously gives rise to a number of questions. For instance, even if the behavioral scientist can control human behavior, how does he, being limited by his own frame

[11]*Ibid.*, p. 175.
[12]*Ibid.*, pp. 204-205.

of reference, know what human behavior ought to be? The scientist may tell us how to perform an abortion, but can he tell us whether or not one ought to be performed? Skinner readily responds to this objection because he is firmly convinced that ethical questions, like all other questions, are to be answered by scientific analysis. He states: "Things are good (positively reinforcing) or bad (negatively reinforcing) presumably because of the contingencies of survival under which the species evolved. . . . All reinforcers eventually derive their power from evolutionary selection."[13] In other words, a thing is good or bad according to whether or not it reinforces behavior that contributes to the survival of the species. This is the ultimate value.

Skinner's thinking is logical, given his presuppositions. But if the God of the Scriptures exists—and He does—the survival of the race is not the chief end of man, nor is it an adequate basis for a value system. Man was made to live for one greater than himself, greater even than the human race. Man was made to live for God. "Whether therefore ye eat, or drink, or whatsoever ye do, do all to the glory of God" (1 Cor. 10:31).

A second and even more threatening question implicit in Skinner's philosophy is: Who is going to design this utopian society? Who among men is qualified for such a task? Dr. Francis A. Schaeffer, trying to imagine the behavioristic scientist at work implementing his utopian dream, writes: "Whom do we find when we get inside of the man with a white lab coat? We find a faulty, lost man, don't we? Where are these great benevolent manipulators going to come from? Talk about utopia! This is the most utopian concept of all."[14]

---

[13]*Ibid.*, p. 99.
[14]Francis A. Schaeffer, *Back to Freedom and Dignity* (London: Hodder and Stoughton, 1973), p. 38.

Moreover, if man is who the behaviorist says he is—namely, an empty organism totally conditioned by his environment—isn't it inconsistent to suggest that human beings (behavioristic scientists) exist who can somehow stand outside this process, intelligently analyzing it and making use of their findings to manipulate the human race in ways of their choosing?

Skinner anticipates this objection. He argues: "The designer of a culture is not an interloper or meddler. He does not step in to disturb a natural process, he is part of a natural process."[15] That is, the person or persons who design the culture are themselves environmentally conditioned to design the culture for the survival of the species. This argument is not very satisfying, even to the man on the street who instinctively views the human being as something more than a machine. The basic weakness with Skinner's position at this point, however, is not his logic but the initial presupposition with which he views the nature of reality. The collision between Christianity and behaviorism begins with their respective starting points.

As I reflect on Skinner's writings, I wonder why he has even bothered to address the general public. His view of mechanical determinism denies that man is in any sense morally responsible. Why does he seek to exhort us and persuade us if we are only machine like men, the product of evolutionary selection and environmental conditioning? Why does he rebuke us for advocating freedom and dignity, if in fact we have no freedom and dignity?

It remains to be seen how much of an impact behaviorism will have on education. If this view is taken seriously by professional educators it will eventually require the construction of schools in which the entire school environment, at every point, reinforces desirable behavior and extinguishes undesirable

[15]Skinner, *op. cit.*, p. 172.

behavior.

The application of Skinner's teaching that has enjoyed by far the most popularity with modern educators is the concept of programmed learning used in conjunction with the teaching machine. Skinner is not the only, or even the first, educational psychologist to make use of this method, but his work certainly has given impetus to a more extensive and varied use of this technique.

Programmed learning, based on the same principles by which a behaviorist teaches a pigeon to peck on a disk or play ping-pong, involves dividing the material to be learned into small pieces of information which are presented visually to the student in a logical series of small steps. The student reads the information in each step and answers a very simple question. The teaching machine informs the student immediately whether or not each answer is correct. Inasmuch as the material is arranged so that the student is likely to make a correct response, there is reinforcement after each small step, and thus motivation to take the next step. This procedure is followed to the end of the program.

As may be expected, researchers are not agreed as to their evaluation of programmed learning. One reason is their lack of agreement on the purpose of education. What is a desirable educational outcome? If the primary purpose of education is the mastery of easily defined factual information as measured by an objective test, then much that is positive can be said for programmed learning. If, on the other hand, the learning objective is that the pupil understand and commit himself to the truth—the result of which cannot be fully measured by objective tests—then teaching machines and programmed learning are of a much more limited value.

The use of an objective test as a criterion for evaluating an instructional approach is in itself subject to question. It may be argued that the ability to recall information for this type of test does not necessarily indicate the ability to apply that information to life situations.

Psychologists recognize the need for more research in assessing the psychological effect of minimal step learning. Borger and Seaborne, after citing a number of possible advantages of programmed learning, give this word of caution:

> There is to date insufficient evidence on the question of whether the response involved in making a large learning step is always equivalent to making a number of small ones. The real situations for which the learner is preparing will certainly involve occasions on which it is necessary to withhold responses until quite a large amount of information has been taken in. In the absence of direct evidence, it may be argued that minimal-step training *may* have disadvantageous second-order effects, in failing to prepare the student for learning situations which cannot be programmed in this way.[16]

From a Christian standpoint, it must be remembered that programmed learning is based on a reductive view of man. It presents reality to him just as an animal trainer presents it to an animal. If this approach is used exclusively, no opportunity is allowed for analysis and interpretation of compelx situations, which man, as man, is called upon to do by the great God who made him.

[16]Robert Borger and A.E.M. Seaborne, *The Psychology of Learning* (Baltimore: Penguin Books, 1966), pp. 211-212.

It must also be remembered that the unregenerate man who rejects God may look at the world in an atomistic and fragmented way. On the other hand, the believer who is self-consciously aware of the implications of his Christian commitment knows that all truth is a unity because God is its Author. For any aspect of reality to be rightly understood, therefore, it must at some point be put in the widest possible context.

The teaching machine, as a part of a comprehensive instructional program, may have value to a Christian educator. But it is not adequate as used alone or as a major element in the educational program to teach the unity of truth to man—a being whom God has made a little lower than the angels and has crowned with glory and honor.

SØREN KIERKEGAARD AND EXISTENTIALISM

Another philosophy that has become popularly acclaimed in this century is existentialism. This philosophy is not a clearly-defined school of thought with all its adherents subscribing generally to the same basic tenets. The term existentialist is applied to men with views as varied as those of Martin Buber, a Jewish theologian, and Jean Paul Sartre, an avowed atheist.

The modern movement called existentialism is usually traced back to Søren Kierkegaard, the nineteenth century Danish philosopher. According to Casserly, the term " 'existentialism' is a modern philosophical term, invented by Kierkegaard and since kept alive by his somewhat mixed band of followers."[17] In a very real sense Kierkegaard stands in a relationship to existentialism as Calvin does to Calvinism.

---

[17]J. V. Langmead Casserly, *The Christian in Philosophy* (New York: Charles Scribner's Sons, 1951), p. 45.

Why should a person interested in education concern himself with Kierkegaard's thought when he wrote no material directly concerned with the problems of education? The reason is that many of our current creative thinkers in art, literature, theology, and to some extent, education, have been significantly influenced by the thought of this Danish philosopher. One might suppose from an examination of recent books and articles in the field of educational philosophy that Soren Kierkegaard may be the catalyst in educational thought in the latter half of this century that John Dewey was in the first.

Søren Kierkegaard was a man with an unusual capacity for suffering, guilt, and inwardness. He was himself very much "the individual," a phrase which refers to the most important category in his thought.[18] This was "the category through which, in a religious respect, this age, all history, the human race as a whole, must pass."[19] So important to him was this category that he expressed the desire "that on my grave might be put 'the individual.' "[20] " 'The individual' " is "a thought in which is contained an entire philosophy of life and of the world."[21]

Kierkegaard did not like systems in general nor the Hegelian system in particular. For him, the thing that really mattered was not the abstract and the general but rather the immediate and the particular. Human existence was not something to be reduced to a concept, either of oneself or of another, but was

---

[18]Søren Kierkegaard, *The Point of View for My Work as an Author, Two Notes About "The Individual," and on My Work as an Author*, translated by Walter Lowrie (London: Oxford University Press, 1939), p. 24.

[19]*Ibid.*, p. 128.

[20]Søren Kierkegaard, *The Journal of Søren Kierkegaard*, a selection edited and translated by Alexander Dru (London: Oxford University Press, 1938), p.

[31]Kierkegaard, *The Point of View*, p. 21.

something to be realized by the individual.

Thus the ontological task, as Kierkegaard saw it, was to describe the individual as he actually exists. He was not looking for some all-encompassing theory to explain man and the world.

With due apologies to Kierkegaard for attempting to systematize some aspects of his thought, I would like to set forth four basic ideas that seem to run through his works, ideas that are also somewhat characteristic of modern day existentialism.

First of all, contrary to traditional philosophies, Kierkegaard believed that existence precedes essence. The existing individual is continually moving from potentiality to actuality through a free, spontaneous, inner act. He is, therefore, never in the position of being finished or complete. An obvious result of this belief is seen in contemporary theologians, psychologists, and educators who speak not of being a self but of becoming a self, not of being a person but of becoming a person. Vandenberg has rightly pointed out: "If, for Dewey, life is experience, which is education, so too is becoming oneself 'education' for the Existentialist."[22]

The existing individual chooses in freedom, and this choice is basic to his being. "The choice itself is decisive for the content of personality," says Kierkegaard; "through the choice the personality immerses itself in the thing chosen, and when it does not choose it withers away in consumption."[23] The existing individual is the architect of his own being and the determiner of his own destiny through the choices that he makes or does not make (also a choice). This view differs radically from

[22]D. Vandenberg, "Experimentalism in the Anesthetic Society Existential Education," *Harvard Educational Review*, XXXii, No. 2 (Spring, 1962), p. 176.

[23]Søren Kierkegaard, *Either/Or*, Vol. II, translated by Walter Lowrie (Princeton: Princeton University Press, 1946), p. 138.

the Christian theistic view of the absolute sovereignty of God, which limits the freedom of man, and from the impersonal mechanical determinism of behaviorism, which denies the freedom of man.

The existentialist goes a step beyond the subjectivism of pragmatism in making educational decisions. The existentialist reasons: "Democratic group decision may be an improvement on dogmatic, authoritarian decision, but it is still inferior to an even more basic level of action—individual decision."[24]

Imagine that you are standing on the edge of a burning building. The fire is moving closer to you. The building is high enough that a jump would involve great risk. You must choose. You must choose to jump into the fire, jump off the building, or remain where you are. Even if you do not choose, that is a choice. It is a choice not to choose. The situation is not static. The fire continues to move closer to you. If it were possible, you could try to think about something else or you could amuse yourself with a game. You could turn up the portable radio a little louder. But if you made an existential choice, you would do so in full awareness of yourself and the crisis situation, taking counsel from nothing outside of yourself.

This was the way Kierkegaard understood the meaning of existence. As Aiken wrote:

We may take him (Kierkegaard) to be saying essentially that only in states of extreme emotional crisis, when one faces not just the possibility but the fact of one's own imminent

[24]Van Cleve Morris, *Philosophy and the American School* (Boston: Houghton Mifflin Company, 1961), pp. 87-88.

annihilation can one finally grasp the significance of one's own existence. For it is only
then that one at last decides to live or die, to be
or not to be.[25]

It is understandable, therefore, why Kierkegaard was preoccupied with those emotions that are related to a crisis situation,
such as anxiety, guilt, fear, dread, boredom, and melancholy.
There was nothing more real to him than his own inner agony.

A second characteristic of existentialism is its emphasis on
the subjectivity of truth. "Truth is subjectivity," declared
Kierkegaard.[26] He then turned the statement around and said,
"Subjectivity is truth."[27] Something is true when it is true for
the individual in his existential situation. It is upon this basic
assumption that Kierkegaard's epistemology rests, although
he made no attempt to develop a formal epistemological
theory.

The subjectivity of truth is indicated in the existentialist's
emphasis upon the "how" rather than the "what" of knowledge. Perhaps in no other place in Kierkegaard's writings is
this point more clearly illustrated than in this often quoted
passage:

If one who lives in the midst of Christendom
goes up to the house of God, the house of the
true God, with the true conception of God in
his knowledge, and prays, but prays in a false

[25]Henry D. Aiken, *The Age of Ideology* (New York: A Mentor Book, Published by
New American Library, 1956), p. 229.
[26]Søren Kierkegaard, *Concluding Unscientific Postscript,* translated by David F.
Swenson (Princeton: Princeton University Press, 1941), p. 169.
[27]*Ibid.*, p. 182.

spirit; and one who lives in an idolatrous community prays with the entire passion of the infinite, although his eyes rest upon the image of an idol: where is there most truth? The one prays in truth to God though he worships an idol; the other prays falsely to the true God, and hence worships in fact an idol.[28]

The test of truth, then, is whether or not a person is passionately committed to it. Early in his career Kierkegaard noted in his *Journals:* "The thing is to find a truth which is true for me, to find the idea for which I can live and die."[29] From this position he never departed. It emerged as characteristic of his thinking and permeated all his writings.

A good example of Kierkegaard's attempt to contrast his approach to reality with traditional philosophy is to be seen in his raising of the question: "When one man investigates objectively the problem of immortality, and another embraces an uncertainty with the passion of the infinite: where is there most truth and who has the greater certainty?"[30] At this point he introduces Socrates as an illustration of the latter alternative and says of his death, "Is any better proof capable of being given for the immortality of the soul?"[31] The point is well taken. Nevertheless, it should be noted here that, as a matter of record, Socrates did offer proofs for the immortality of the soul of the type that Kierkegaard so bitterly condemns. One could conclude that it was Socrates' conviction that these proofs were valid that enabled him to meet death in such a

---

[28]*Ibid.*, pp. 179-180.
[29]Kierkegaard, *Journals*, p. 15.
[30]Kierkegaard, *Postscript,* p. 180.
[31]*Ibid.*

noble manner.

Before leaving the topic of the subjectivity of truth, a legitimate question may be raised, especially by the educator who is very much concerned with the task of communication. If truth is subjective, how can any truth, even this truth, be communicated? When one writes as his own view the statement "Truth is subjective," he is involved in a contradiction. Kierkegaard was well aware of this problem and advocated the use of indirect communication. Even this proposition involved him in the same problem.

In all fairness to Kierkegaard, however, he was a gifted writer and often was very artful in the use of indirect communication. The use of double reflection is quite evident in his writings. The following is a good example:

> Suppose a man wished to communicate the conviction that the God-relationship of the individual is a secret. Suppose he were what we are accustomed to call a kindly soul, who loved others so much that he simply could not keep this to himself; suppose he nevertheless had sense enough to feel a little of the contradiction involved in communicating it directly, and hence told it to others only under a pledge of secrecy: what then? Then he must either have assumed that the disciple was wiser than his teacher, so that he could really keep the secret while the teacher could not (beautiful satire upon being a teacher!); or he must have become so overwhelmed with the bliss of galimatias that he did not notice the contradiction.[32]

[32]*Ibid.*, p. 72.

Educators influenced by existentialism would be likely to prefer symbolism to literalism, provocative questions to direct exposition, and poetry to prose. In every case the question is: "What does it mean to you?" and not, "What does it mean?"

By Kierkegaard's standards, humanly speaking, Socrates was the outstanding example of an authentic individual skilled in the art of indirect communication. Socrates' method consisted of posing penetrating questions in such a way as to force the learner to face squarely both the issue and himself in depth. He made no formal speeches. He even went to the point of feigning ignorance in order to avoid giving answers and to elicit ideas from the person to whom he was talking. Interestingly enough, to the extent that Socrates occasionally injected information into the stream of conversation, Kierkegaard believed him to be inconsistent.[33]

A third characteristic of Kierkegaard's thought that is also common to modern existentialism is the concept of paradox. This concept logically follows from Kierkegaard's view of reality and the nature of truth. He wrote: "Paradox is not a concession but a category, an ontological definition which expresses the relation between an existing cognitive spirit and eternal truth."[34] All essential truth is paradoxical from the standpoint of the existing individual, and any attempt to explain the paradox rationally is to deny the reality of existence. According to Kierkegaard the paradox bring some to despair because the antitheses cannot be bridged by human thought. Reason can only discern the members of the paradox; it cannot reconcile them.

But what reason cannot do, faith can. Thus we have the leap of faith. Faith is operative "by virtue of the absurd, not by vir-

[33]*Ibid.*, p. 247.
[34]Kierkegaard, *Journals,* p. 194.

tue of the human understanding, otherwise it is merely worldly wisdom, not faith."[35] This leads inevitably to the irrationalism of modern existentialism.

I had a friend in seminary who was very much influenced by existentialist irrationalism as expressed in neo-orthodox theology. He was a brilliant student. We often engaged in theological arguments, sometimes for hours at a time. On rare occasions I would get the better of the argument, and I would say to him, "Now I have you. What you are saying logically contradicts what you have been saying." His inevitable reply was, "But that is just the point. You see, I contend that truth may be illogical." At this juncture the incompatibility of our starting points would become painfully evident, and in frustration we would go our separate ways.

In a much more radical and tragic way, modern man seems to be saying through the various art forms and the mass media that the only way an earthbound existence makes any sense is to say that it doesn't make any sense. The only way man can retain his sanity is to recognize that life is absurd.

A fourth characteristic of Kierkegaard's thought that will be considered is his emphasis on authentic existence. For him, good and evil are not fixed values nor are they to be measured in terms of some absolute, objective, moral prescription. The pivotal ethical question is whether or not an individual is in an authentic or inauthentic mode of existence. To have authentic existence is for one to choose himself as he really is, with all of his traits, no matter what they may be.[36] The choice is up to the individual. The real hero for Kierkegaard was "the man who can really stand alone in the world only taking counsel from his conscience."[37]

[35]*Ibid.,* p. 122.
[36]Kierkegaard, *Either/Or,* p. 1210.
[37]Kierkegaard, *Journals,* p. 416.

Vandenberg, writing from an existentialist position, says that if a student cheats on an examination, "it is either the result of the student's inauthenticity (he is not being what he can be, he does not want to become a 'trouble maker')" or on the other hand, "it is the result of his authenticity (he is being what he chooses to be which happens to run counter to prevailing modes of conduct, he wants to be a 'trouble maker')."[38]

What then should the teacher do? When he is giving an examination, what course should he follow with regard to cheating? The existentialist answers, "The teacher cannot stand in the way of the crisis without causing inauthenticity and setting the scene for future discipline problems."[39] The only thing the teacher can do is to "clarify the situation by rendering explicit the choice at hand. The student chooses for himself to become what he can become."[40] The teacher's duty with respect to discipline, therefore, is twofold: "to be himself and to let the student be himself."[41]

The Christian theist shares the existentialist's concern for honesty. Hypocrisy is one of the greatest evils of this and every other time. But authenticity is not enough. A person can be authentically depraved.

It may be that you have never seen any one of the above philosophies implemented consistently in church or school education. You may be assured, however, that wherever formal education is taking place, it is being done according to an educational philosophy. It may be conscious or unconscious. It may be pragmatic, behavioristic, existentialist, or eclectic—or it could be Christian.

[38]Vandenberg, *op. cit.*, p. 184.
[39]*Ibid.*
[40]*Ibid.*
[41]*Ibid.*

APPENDIX A

A CHRISTIAN EDUCATOR'S CREED

THE BASIS OF AN EDUCATIONAL CREED

1. All human thought rightly begins with the sovereign, triune God. A Chrisitan view of reality is a God-centered view of reality.

2. Everything comes from God, is sustained by Him, and is directed to His glory (Rom. 11:36).

3. God has given man in the Holy Scripture an infallible, transcendent norm by which all of life is to be understood truly and governed rightly.

4. An educational creed must be supplementary to, but consistent with, one's confession of faith. This writer believes that the Westminister Confession of Faith contains the system of doctrine taught in the Holy Scripture.

A STATEMENT OF BELIEF CONCERNING THE NATURE OF EDUCATION

Education is the conscious and purposeful process by which a person comes to understand, love, and commit himself to the truth through teaching and study. Education is both an operative and cooperative process. On the one hand, the teacher directs and corrects the pupil on the basis of a norm which transcends the pupil's experience. On the other hand, the teacher cooperates with the divinely ordained laws of child growth by addressing himself to the unfolding spiritual, intellectual, physical, emotional, and social needs of the student.

A STATEMENT OF BELIEF CONCERNING
THE ESSENTIAL FACTORS OF EDUCATION

1. **The teacher.** The Christian teacher is one who is called by God to the ministry of teaching. His task is to equip the student for his calling in life. He carries out his work through a kingly, prophetic, and priestly function. The teacher cannot learn for the student, but compelled by the love of Christ, he pours out his life in an effort to inspire the student to fulfill his responsibility in the learning process.

2. **The student.** The student has a divinely ordained task. As one made in the image of God, he has both the capacity and the responsibility for active involvement in the teaching-learning process. Although the image of God was broken in the fall of man, it was not eradicated. The student's life, therefore, is still precious. He has a potential that cannot be measured by human instruments. His deepest need is to be brought into a right relationship with Jesus Christ; his highest goal is to serve the Lord in all of life.

   The whole person is made in the image of God and it is the whole person on which the teaching-learning process must focus.

3. **Objectives.** The comprehensive objective of education is to glorify God. All other objectives are subordinate to this end. Objectives should be stated in a manner consistent with the nature of the activity to which they are applied; i. e. inasmuch as the learner is a rational and moral being, objectives that pertain to learning should be stated in cognitive and volitional terms. Some objectives are measurable (to be able to recite ten lines of poetry); some are immeasurable (to know the power of the resurrection).

Some objectives are attainable (to add five new classrooms this year); some are unattainable, at least in this life (to be perfectly holy). Yet all of the above may be used in some way to give direction, to encourage concentration of effort, and to provide a basis for evaluation.

4. **The curriculum.** The curriculum is God-centered. It is shaped by the Word of God, a norm which transcends both the content of the arts and sciences and the experience of the individual learner. The cumulative experience of the race, as well as the particular experiences of the individual, stand under the judgment of Scripture. Only from this vantage point can a curriculum be designed that will truly reflect the structure of knowledge and at the same time adequately provide for the real needs of the student.

   A God-centered curriculum is of necessity an integrated curriculum. All the diverse areas of knowledge, including the content of the curriculum, have their unity in God, Who is the source of all truth.

5. **Teaching method.** The redeemed personality of the Christian teacher is the human instrument through which truth is communicated. Instructional techniques such as lecture, discussion, and role-playing may be learned by study, observation, and practice, but they become operative only through the personality of the teacher.

   Method is a means to the end of communicating truth. It is never an end in itself.

6. **The Christian school.** A Christian school is a Christian academic community with the distinctive task of equipping students individually and corporately to exercise dominion in Christ over all that He has made.

APPENDIX B

HOW TO START A CHRISTIAN SCHOOL

The procedure for starting a Christian school will vary according to the type of school desired (i. e., parochial, parent-controlled, proprietary, non-profit corporation) in addition to other factors. The following suggestions should be adaptable to most situations.

1. Seek out others who share your burden for Christian education. Meet with them on a regular basis for prayer, for becoming better informed about Christian education, and for discussing ways of generating a broader base of interest in the community.

2. Develop a structure.
   a. A sponsoring body should appoint a committee to make a feasibility study. The study should include a determination of the need for a Christian school in the community, an assessment of support, and an investigation into the availability of facilities. The feasibility committee should make its report to the sponsoring body.
   b. If the feasibility committee's report is favorable, the sponsoring body should elect a board of trustees. A five to seven member board is recommended. Each member should be a mature Christian committed to the need for a Christian school. It would be wise to include on the board a lawyer and an accountant. If the sponsoring body does not wish to include women on the board, it would be advisable to set up an advisory committee of two or three mothers. It is important for the board to have the input of those who send the children off to school every day. Having parents on the board is desirable, but it should not be a prerequisite for membership.

3. Lay the foundations. The board of trustees, with the counsel of a professional Christian educator, should do the following:

a. Draw up a constitution and by-laws. (Models are available from Christian school associations.)* These documents should be approved by the sponsoring body. (Some may prefer the use of a steering committee to draft the constitution and by-laws prior to the election of the board). This foundation should be laid carefully and observed strictly in actual practice.

b. Decide on the number of grades to be included in the initial operation of the school. Some schools begin with a kindergarten and add one grade per year. If there is sufficient interest, the school could begin with kindergarten through third grade, or in the case of considerable support, kindergarten through sixth. Building soundly, however, is more important than building quickly.

c. Prepare a tentative budget. Income should be based on tuition from anticipated enrollment. The Christian community as a whole should be made aware of its obligation to give financial support to the school. This practice would make scholarship aid available and reduce the financial burden on the Christian parent. In most cases there is no way, humanly speaking, to have a Christian school without supporters (both those who have children in school and those who do not) who are willing to give sacrificially of themselves and their money.

d. Develop policies and procedures for the admission of students. What criteria will be used for the admission of students? If there is a waiting list, will there be an order of preference for accepting students other than the date of application? If so, what will be the basis for making this determination? Prepare an application form. (Models may be obtained from Christian school associations.)* Be sure to include on the form a statement indicating the parent's willingness to have his child receive a distinctively Christian education.

4. Make a public announcement of the opening of the school, inviting the Christian community to make application for admission. This announcement should be made by February 1st before the school year begins in September. The decision to begin is the most difficult step of all. Only in rare situations will sufficient enrollment and adequate income be assured prior to the time when the commitment to announce the opening has to be made. In almost every case when a Christian school is established there has to come that time when those in authority are willing to step out in faith.

5. Once the commitment has been made to open the school, a number of actions need to be taken.
   a. The board should secure a headmaster. In cases where there are only two or three teachers in the school, one of the teachers could assume this responsibility in addition to his regular duties. The direction of the school will be shaped more by this individual than by any other human factor. Great care, therefore, should be taken in the selection process.
   b. The headmaster should employ a secretary. The secretary comes into more frequent contact with the patrons than any other staff member. In addition to the usual secretarial skills, she should be able to meet people well and, most of all, she should have a strong commitment to the purpose of the school. In the beginning a part-time worker could be used.
   c. Upon authorization by the board, the headmaster should proceed to hire a faculty. What formal education

means to a child will depend more upon the teacher than any other factor. The administration must give the highest priority to the kind of faculty it brings to the students. Some of the questions the headmaster would want to have answered about the prospective teacher are: Is he a mature Christian? Is he academically competent? Can he relate his faith to his task as a teacher? What are his reasons for seeking the particular position for which he is applying? How does he feel about children? Does he have a sincere interest in teaching?

d. Select and purchase textbooks. At the present time quality textbooks written by Christian scholars are available in only a few areas of the curriculum. Each prospective textbook should be evaluated critically. Some teachers may be equipped to prepare their own printed materials. (A curriculum guide with textbook recommendations may be obtained from Christian school associations.)* The textbooks can be purchased by the school and rented to the student at a moderate cost that would allow the school to turn over the books on an average of every four years.

e. Secure adequate facilities. Minimum building requirements for a K-3 program with one hundred pupils would include four classrooms (approximately 500 sq. ft. each) and space for an office. Approximately five acres are recommended for playground area. It is entirely possible that the facilities of a local church meet, or could be made to meet, these requirements.

6. Provide a two or three day workshop for faculty and staff just prior to the opening of the school. The integration of faith and learning would be an appropriate topic to consider.

7. Set aside a morning for the orientation and registration of pupils.

8. Begin the first day of classes.

*Additional information on the starting and operation of a Christian school may be obtained by writing a Christian school association: The names and addresses of the three of the associations with which I am familiar are as follows:

Association of Christian Schools International
P. O. Box 4097
Whittier, California 90607

Christian Schools International
3350 East Paris Avenue, SE
Grand Rapids, Michigan 49508

Southern Association of Christian Schools
3005 Highwy 280 South
Birmingham, Alabama 35243

APPENDIX C

SUGGESTED BOOKS FOR USE IN THE TRAINING OF TEACHERS
AND ADMINISTRATORS IN CHURCH EDUCATION

BIBLE

OLD TESTAMENT SURVEY

DeGraaf, S. G. *Promise and Deliverance: From Creation to the Conquest of Canaan,* Vol. I. Philadelphia: Presbyterian and Reformed Publishing Company, 1977.

DeGraaf, S. G. *Promise and Deliverance: The Failure of Israel's Theocracy,* Vol. II. St. Catharines, Ontario: Paideia Press, 1978.

Scott, Jack B. *God's Plan Unfolded.* Wheaton: Tyndale House Publishers, 1978.

NEW TESTAMENT SURVEY

DeGraaf, S. G. *Promise and Deliverance: Christ's Ministry and Death,* Vol. III. St. Catharines, Ontario: Paideia Press, 1979.

Tenney, Merrill C. *New Testament Survey.* Grand Rapids: William B. Eerdmans Publishing Company, 1961.

UNDERSTANDING THE BIBLE

A. Principles of Interpretation

Sproul, R. C. *Knowing Scripture.* Downers Grove, Illinois: InterVarsity Press, 1977.

B. Methods of Bible Study

Richards, L. O. *Creative Bible Study.* Grand Rapids: Zondervan Publishing House, 1971.

Vos, Howard F. *Effective Bible Study.* Grand Rapids: Zondervan Publishing House, 1956.

Wald, Oletta. *The Joy of Discovery in Bible Study.* Minneapolis: Augsburg Publishing House, 1975.

CHRISTIAN DOCTRINE

Berkhof, Louis. *Manual of Christian Doctrine.* Grand Rapids: William B. Eerdmans Publishing Company, 1933.

Packer, J. I. *Fundamentalism and the Word of God.* Grand Rapids: William B. Eerdmans Publishing Company, 1958.

Packer, J. I. *Knowing God.* Downers Grove: InterVarsity Press, 1973.
Stott, John R. W. *Basic Christianity.* Downers Grove: InterVarsity Press, 1954.

CHURCH HISTORY

WORLD

Jackson, Jeremy C. *No Other Foundation - The Church Through Twenty Centuries.* Westchester, Illinois: Cornerstone Books, 1980.

UNITED STATES

Woodbridge, John D., Mark A. Noll and Nathan O. Hatch *The Gospel in America - Themes in the Story of America's Evangelicals.* Grand Rapids: Zondervan Publishing House, 1979.

DENOMINATIONAL

Carlson, Paul. *Our Presbyterian Heritage.* Elgin, Illinois: David C. Cook Publishing Company, 1973.

Cole, Edward B. *Our Baptist Heritage.* Elgin, Illinois: David C. Cook Publishing Company, 1973.

Howe, John W. *Our Anglican Heritage.* Elgin, Illinois: David C. Cook Publishing Company, 1973.

Keysor, Charles W. *Our Methodist Heritage.* Elgin, Illinois: David C. Cook Publishing Company, 1973.

CHRISTIAN EDUCATION

CHRISTIAN PHILOSOPHY OF EDUCATION

A. Christian World and Life View

Sire, James W. *The Universe Next Door.* Downers Grove: InterVarsity Press, 1976.

B. Application of a Christian World and Life View to Education

DeJong, Norman. *Education in the Truth.* Philadelphia: Presbyterian and Reformed Publishing Company, 1969.

Harper, Norman E. *Making Disciples - The Challenge of Christian Education at the End of the Twentieth Century.* Memphis: Christian Studies Center, 1981.

AGE GROUPS - HUMAN GROWTH & DEVELOPMENT, TEACHING - LEARNING PROCESS, PROGRAMS

A. Children

Bolton, Barbara J. *Ways to Help Them Learn: Children -grades 1 to 6.* Glendale, California: Regal Books, 1972.

Haystead, Wesley. *You Can't Begin Too Soon.* Glendale, California: Regal Books, 1974.

Rowen, Dolores. *Ways to Help Them Learn: Early Childhood - birth to 5 yrs.* Glendale, California: Regal Books, 1972.

Zuck, Roy B. and Robert E. Clark *Childhood Education in the Church.* Chicago: Moody Press, 1975.

B. Youth

Irving, Roy G. *Youth and the Church.* Chicago: Moody Press, 1968.

Richards, L. O. *Youth Ministry.* Grand Rapids: Zondervan Publishing House, 1972.

Zuck, Roy B. and Waren S. Bevion, (eds.) *Youth Education in the Church.* Chicago: Moody Press, 1978.

C. Adults

Wright, N. H. *Ways to Help Them Learn.* Glendale, California: Regal Books, 1971.

Zuck, Roy B. and Gene A. Getz, eds. *Adult Education in the Church.* Chicago: Moody Press, 1970.

TEACHING METHODS

Edge, Finley B. *Helping the Teacher.* Nashville: Broadman Press, 1959.

Gregory, John Milton. *Seven Laws of Teaching.* Grand Rapids: Baker Book House, 1954.

Richards, L. O. *Creative Bible Teaching.* Chicago: Moody Press, 1970.

ADMINISTRATION OF CHURCH EDUCATION

Bower, Robert K. *Administering Christian Education.* Grand Rapids: William B. Eerdmans, 1964.

Gangel, Kenneth O. *Leadership for Church Education.* Chicago: Moody Press, 1970.

Lebar, Lois. *Focus on People in Church Education.* Nashville: Fleming H. Revell Company, 1968.

PRACTICAL THEOLOGY

COUNSELING

Adams, Jay. *Competent to Counsel.* Phillipsburg, New Jersey: Presbyterian and Reformed Publishing Co., 1970.

Crabb, L. J. *Basic Principles of Biblical Counseling.* Grand Rapids: Zonderman Publishing House, 1975.

EVANGELISM

Kennedy, D. James. *Evangelism Explosion.* Third edition. Wheaton: Tyndale House, 1970.

Kuiper, R. B. *God-Centered Evangelism.* Grand Rapids: Baker Book Co., 1961.

BIBLIOGRAPHY

Adams, Jay E. *Competent to Counsel.* Phillipsburg, New Jersey: Presbyterian and Reformed Publishing Co., 1970.

Aiken, Henry D. *The Age of Ideology.* New York: A Mentor Book, published by New American Library, 1956.

Armbruster, Frank E. "The More We Spend, The Less Children Learn," *The Compact New York Times Magazine.* (August 28, 1977): 81-82.

Armerding, Hudson T., ed. *Christianity and the World of Thought.* Chicago: Moody Press, 1968.

Augustine. *The First Catechetical Instruction.* Translated by Joseph P. Christopher. New York: Newman Press, 1946.

————. *The Teacher.* Washington: Catholic University Press, 1968.

Babbage, Stuart B. *Christianity and Sex.* Chicago: InterVarsity Press, 1963.

Barclay, William. *Educational Ideals in the Ancient World.* Grand Rapids: Baker Book House, 1974. (Formerly printed under the title *Train Up a Child.*)

Bavinck, Herman. *Our Reasonable Faith.* Grand Rapids: Wm. B. Eerdmans Publishing Co., 1956.

Baxter, Richard. *Plain Scripture Proof on Infant Church-Membership and Baptism.* London: Robert White, 1651.

Bayh, Birch. "Seeking Solutions to School Violence and Vandalism," *Phi Delta Kappan 59* (January 1978): 300-301.

Bebbington, D. W. *Patterns in History: A Christian View.* Downers Grove: InterVarsity Press, 1979.

Benson, C. H. *Popular History of Christian Education.* Chicago: Moody Press, 1943.

Berkhof, Louis. "The Covenant of Grace and Its Significance for Christian Education," *Fundamentals in Christian Education,* ed. by Cornelius Jaarsma. Grand Rapids: Wm. B. Eerdmans Publishing Co., 1953.

Beth, Marc. *Education as a Discipline.* Boston: Allyn and Bacon, 1965.

Beversluis, N. H. *Christian Philosophy of Education.* Grand Rapids: National Union of Christian Schools, 1971.

Blamires, Harry. *The Christian Mind.* New York: Seabury Press, 1963.

Blumenfeld, Samuel L. *How to Start Your Own Private School - And Why You Need One.* New York: Arlington House, 1972.

Boehlke, Robert R. *Theories of Learning in Christian Education.* Philadelphia: The Westminster Press, 1962.

Boeve, Edgar. *Children's Art and the Christian Teacher.* St. Louis: Concordia Publishing House, 1966.

The Book of Church Order of the Presbyterian Church in the United States. Richmond, Virginia: The Board of Christian Education, The General Assembly of the P.C.U.S.

Borger, Robert, and A.E.M. Seaborne. *The Psychology of Learning.* Baltimore: Penguin Books, 1966.

Bower, Robert K. *Administering Christian Education.* Grand Rapids: Wm. B. Eerdmans Publishing Co., 1964.

Brederveld, Jakob. *Christian Education: A Summary and Critical Discussion of Bavinck's Pedagogical Principles.* Grand Rapids: Smitter Book Co., 1928.

Brekke, Milo. *How Different Are People Who Attended Lutheran Schools.* St. Louis: Concordia Publishing House, 1974.

Bromiley, G. W. *Children of Promise.* Grand Rapids: Wm. B. Eerdmans Publishing Co., 1979.

Browning, Robert. "Rabbi Ben Ezra," *The Literature of England: An Anthology and A History,* Vol. II, ed., by George B. Woods, Homer A. Watt, and George K. Anderson, 3rd ed. Chicago: Scott, Foresman, and Co., 1948.

Bruner, Jerome S. *Toward a Theory of Instruction.* Cambridge: Belknap Press, 1966.

Buchanan, Henry A., and Bob W. Brown. "Will Protestant Christian Schools Become a Third Force?" *Christianity Today 11* (May 1967): 3.

Bushnell, Horace. *Christian Nurture.* New Haven: Yale University Press, 1967.

Butler, James D. *Four Philosophies and their Practice in Education and Religion.* New York: Harper and Row, 1968.

Calvin, John. *Institutes of the Christian Religion.* Translated by Henry Beveridge, Vol. I. Grand Rapids: Wm. B. Eerdmans Publishing Co., 1962.

Casserly, J. V. Langmead. *The Christian in Philosophy.* New York: Charles Scribner's Sons, 1951.

Christenson, Larry. *The Christian Family.* Minneapolis: Bethany Fellowship, 1970.

Christian Liberal Arts Education. Report of the Calvin College Curriculum Study Committee, 1970.

Clark, Gordon H. *A Christian Philosophy of Education.* Grand Rapids: Wm. B. Eerdmans Publishing Co., 1946.

Committee of Phi Delta Kappa, E. A. Lee, chairman. "Teaching as a Man's Job," *Phi Delta Kappa.* (Homewood, Illinois: 1958), p. 56.

Committee on Religion and Education. *The Function of the Public Schools in Dealing with Religion.* Washington, D.C.: American Council on Education, 1953.

Course of Study for Christian Schools. Grand Rapids: Wm. B. Eerdmans Publishing Co., 1953.

Cubberly, Ellwood P. *Readings in the History of Education.* Boston: Houghton Mifflin Co., 1920.

Cully, Iris V. and Kendig Brubaker Cully, eds. *Process and Relationship.* Birmingham: Religious Education Press, 1978.

Cully, Kendig Brubaker. *Basic Writings in Christian Education.* Philadelphia: Westminster Press, 1960.

_____. *The Search for a Christian Education Since 1940.* Westminster Press, 1965.

_____. ed. *The Westminster Dictionary of Christian Education.* Philadelphia: The Westminster Press, 1963.

Culver, R. D. "Matthew 28:16–20," *Bulletin of the Evangelical Theological Society 10* (Spring 1967): 115-126.

Cummings, David B., ed. *The Purpose of a Christian School.* Phillipsburg, New Jersey: Presbyterian and Reformed Publishing Co., 1979.

DeGraaff, A. H. *The Educational Ministry of the Church.* Free University of Amsterdam, 1966.

DeGraaff, A. H. and Jean Olthius. *Joy in Learning.* Toronto: Curriculum Development Centre, 1971.

DeJong, Norman. *Education in the Truth.* Philadelphia: Presbyterian and Reformed Publishing Co., 1969.

_____. *Philosophy of Education: A Christian Approach.* Nutley, New Jersey: Presbyterian and Reformed Publishing Co., 1977.

Delitzsch, Franz. *Biblical Commentary on the Proverbs of Solomon,* Vol. II. Grand Rapids: Wm. B. Eerdmans Publishing Co., 1968.

Dewey, John. "My Pedagogic Creed," *John Dewey on Education,* ed. by Reginald D. Archambault. New York: The Modern Library, 1964.

_____. *A Common Faith.* New Haven: Yale University Press, 1934.

_____. *Democracy and Education.* New York: Free Press, 1916.

Dobson, James. *Dare to Discipline.* Wheaton: Tyndale House Publishers, 1970.

Dodd, C. H. *The Apostolic Preaching and Its Developments.* London: Hodder and Stoughton Ltd., 1944.

Eastwood, Cyril. *The Priesthood of All Believers.* Minneapolis: Augsburg Publishing House, 1916.

Eavey, C. B. *History of Christian Education.* Chicago: Moody Press, 1964.

_____. *Principles of Teaching for Christian Teachers.* Grand Rapids: Zondervan Publishing House, 1940.

Eby, Frederick. *Early Protestant Educators.* New York: A.M.S. Press, 1971.

Edge, Findley B. *Helping the Teacher.* Nashville: Broadman Press, 1959.

186

Edwards, Newton, and Herman G. Richey. *The School in the American Social Order.* Boston: Houghton Mifflin Co., 1947.

Elliot, Harrison S. *Can Religious Education Be Christian?* New York. The Macmillan Co., 1949.

Fairchild, Roy W. *Christians in Families.* Richmond: C.L.C. Press, 1964.

Fakkema, Mark. *Christian Philosophy: Its Educational Implications.* Chicago: National Associaton of Christian Schools, 1953.

_____ . "The Organization of the Local Parent-Society Christian School Plant." *Course of Study for Christian Schools.* Grand Rapids: Wm. B. Eerdmans Publishing Co., 1947.

Fennema, Jack. *Nurturing Children in the Lord.* Phillipsburg, New Jersey: Presbyterian and Reformed Publishing Co., 1977.

Ferre, Nels F.S. *A Theology for Christian Education.* Philadelphia: The Westminster Press, 1967.

Feucht, Oscar. *Helping Families Through the Church.* St. Louis: Concordia Publishing House, 1957.

Gaebelein, Frank E. *Christian Education in a Democracy.* New York: Oxford University Press, 1951.

_____ . *The Pattern of God's Truth.* Chicago: Moody Press, 1968.

Gangel, Kenneth O. *Leadership for Church Education.* Chicago: Moody Press, 1970.

Gettys, Joseph M. *Teaching Others How to Teach the Bible.* Richmond: John Knox Press, 1961.

Glen, J. Stanley. *The Recovery of the Teaching Ministry.* Philadelphia: The Westminster Press, 1960.

Gogdill, Olive. "Now It's Goodbye to Dick and Jane Stories," *The Clarion Ledger-Jackson Daily News,* Sunday, July 14, 1974, Section G., p. 1.

Green, J. B. *Studies in the Holy Spirit.* New York: Fleming H. Revell, 1936.

Gregory, John Milton. *Seven Laws of Teaching.* Grand Rapids: Baker Book House, 1954.

Gwynn, Price H., Jr. *Leadership Education in the Local Church.* Philadelphia: The Westminster Press, 1952.

Hakes, J. Edward. *An Introduction to Evangelical Christian Education.* Chicago: Moody Press, 1964.

Hart, Harold H., compiler. *Summerhill: For and Against.* New York: Pocket Books, 1978.

Haystead, Wesley. *Ways to Plan and Organize Your Sunday School.* Glendale: Gospel Light, 1971.

Haystead, Wesley. *You Can't Begin Too Soon.* Glendale, California: International Center for Learning, 1974.

Hefley, James C. *Are Textbooks Harming Your Children?* Milford: Mott Media, 1979.

Henderlite, Rachel. *Forgiveness and Hope: Toward a Theology for Protestant Christian Education.* Richmond: John Knox Press, 1961.

Henderson, Robert W. *The Teaching Office in the Reformed Tradition.* Philadelphia: Westminster Press, 1962.

Henry, Carl F. H. *Aspects of Christian Social Ethics.* Grand Rapids: Wm. B. Eerdmans Publishing Co., 1964.

Hill, Brian V. *Called To Teach.* Sydney, Australia: Angus and Robertson, 1971.

Hodge, A. A. *Popular Lectures on Theological Themes.* Philadelphia: Presbyterian Board of Publication and Sabbath-School Work, 1887.

Hoeksema, Gertrude. *Peaceable Fruit.* Grand Rapids: Reformed Free Publishing Association, 1974.

Hoekstra, Dennis and Arnold De Graaff. *Contrasting Christian Approaches to Teaching Religion and Biblical Studies.* Calvin College Monograph, 1973.

Holmes, Arthur F. *All Truth is God's Truth.* Grand Rapids: Wm. B. Eerdmans Publishing Co., 1977.

_____. *The Idea of a Christian College.* Grand Rapids: Wm. B. Eerdmans Publishing Co., 1975.

Hoogstra, Jacob T., ed. *John Calvin Contemporary Prophet.* Grand Rapids: Wm. B. Eerdmans Publishing Co., 1953.

Horne, Herman H. *Jesus The Master Teacher.* Grand Rapids: Kregel Publications, 1964.

_____. *The Philosophy of Christian Education.* New York: Fleming H. Revell Co., 1937.

Horton, Mrs. Frank C. *How to Teach the Catechism to Children.* Carrollton, Mississippi: Covenant Presbytery Christian Education Committee, 1979.

Howe, George, ed. and trans. *St. Augustine on Education.* South Bend, Indiana: Gateway Editions, Ltd., 1969.

Hugen, Melvin D. *The Church's Ministry to the Older Unmarried.* Grand Rapids: Wm. B. Eerdmans Publishing Co., 1959.

Hurley, Mark J. *Declaration on Christian Education of Vatican Council II.* Glen Rock, New Jersey: Paulist Press, 1966.

Hylkema, G. W. "The Great Office of the Teacher in Preparing the Child for the Complete Life," *Fundamentals in Christian Education,* ed. by Cornelius Jaarsma. Grand Rapids: Wm. B. Eerdmans Publishing Co., 1953.

Illich, Ivan D. *Deschooling Society.* New York: Harper and Row, 1971.

Irving, Roy G. *Youth and the Church.* Chicago: Moody Press, 1968.

Jaarsma, Cornelius. *The Educational Philosophy of Herman Bavinck.* Grand Rapids: Wm. B. Eerdmans Publishing Co., 1935.

————. *Fundamentals in Christian Education, Theory and Practice.* Wm. B. Eerdmans, 1953.

————. *Human Development, Learning and Teaching.* Wm. B. Eerdmans Publishing Co., 1959.

Jahsmann, Allan Hart. *What's Lutheran in Education.* St. Louis: Concordia Publishing House, 1960.

Jewett, Paul K. *Infant Baptism and the Covenant of Grace.* Grand Rapids: Wm. B. Eerdmans Publishing Company, 1978.

Jones, George E. "On Opening Day America's Schools Ponder Some Sobering Lessons," *U.S. News and World Report 83* (September 12, 1977): 29, 81.

Kienel, Paul A. *The Philosophy of Christian School Education.* Association of Christian Schools International, 1978.

Kierkegaard, Søren. *Concluding Unscientific Postscript.* Translated by David F. Swenson. Princeton: Princeton University Press, 1941.

————. *Either/Or,* Vol. II. Translated by Walter Lowrie. Princeton: Princeton University Press, 1946.

————. *The Journals of Søren Kierkegaard.* Edited and translated by Alexander Dru. London: Oxford University Press, 1938.

————. *The Point of View for My Work as an Author, Two Notes About "The Individual," and on My Work as an Author.* Translated by Walter Lowrie. Oxford University Press, 1939.

Kik, J. Marcellus. *The Supreme Court and Prayer in the Public School.* Phillipsburg, New Jersey: Presbyterian and Reformed Publishing Co., 1963.

Kittel, Gerhard, ed. *Theological Dictionary of the New Testament,* Vols. IV, V. Grand Rapids: Wm. B. Eerdmans Publishing Co., 1967.

Kuyper, Abraham. *Christianity as a Life-System: The Witness of a World-View.* Memphis: Christian Studies Center, 1980.

Lange, John Peter. *Commentary on the Holy Scriptures,* Vol. 8. Grand Rapids: Zondervan Publishing House, 1960.

Latourette, Kenneth Scott. *A History of Christianity.* New York: Harper and Brothers, 1953.

LeBar, Lois E. *Education That Is Christian.* Nashville: Fleming H. Revell Co., 1958.

_____ . *Focus on People in Church Education*. Nashville: Fleming H. Revell Co., 1968.

Lee, James Michael. *The Religious Education We Need*. Mishawaka, Indiana: Religious Education Press, 1977.

Liston, R.T.L. *The Neglected Educational Heritage of Southern Presbyterians*. Bristol, Tennessee: Privately printed, n.d.

Lockerbie, D. Bruce. *The Way They Should Go*. Oxford University Press, 1972.

Lowrie, Roy W. *Christian School Administration*. Wheaton: National Association of Christian Schools, 1966.

Lucas, Christopher J. *Our Western Educational Heritage*. New York: The Macmillan Co., 1972.

Lynn, Robert W., and Elliott Wright. *The Big Little School*. New York: Harper and Row, 1971.

McCarthy, Rockne M., James W. Skillen and William A. Harper. *Disestablishment a Second Time: Public Justice for American Schools*. Souix Center, Iowa: Unpublished manuscript.

McQuilkin, J. Robertson. "The Behavioral Sciences Under the Authority of Scripture." *Journal of the Evangelical Society 20* (March 1977): 31–43.

Maatman, Russell and Bakker, Gerald. *Contrasting Christian Approaches to Teaching the Sciences*. Calvin College Monograph, 1971.

Marcel, Pierre. *The Biblical Doctrine of Infant Baptism*. London: James Clarke and Co., Ltd., 1953.

Marique, P. *History of Christian Education* (3 volumes). New York: Fordham University Press, 1924-32.

Maritain, Jacques. *Education at the Crossroads*. New Haven: Yale University Press, 1943.

Marsden, George. *A Christian View of History?* Grand Rapids: Wm. B. Eerdmans Publishing Co., 1975.

May, Phillip. *Which Way to Education*. Chicago: Moody Press, 1975.

Mayer, Marvin K. and others. *Reshaping Evangelical Higher Education*. Grand Rapids: Zondervan Publishing House, 1972.

Meeter, Merle and Stanley Wiersina. *Contrasting Christian Approaches to Teaching Literature*. Calvin College Monograph, 1970.

Mensing, Morella. *Today's Christian Kindergarten*. St. Louis: Concordia Publishing Co., 1972.

Miller, Randolph Crump. *Christian Nurture and the Church*. New York: Charles Scribner's Sons, 1961.

_____ . *The Clue to Christian Education*. Charles Scribner's Sons, 1950.

Moore, Opal. *Why Johnny Can't Learn*. Milford: Mott Media, 1975.

Morris, Henry M. *Education for the Real World.* San Diego: Creation Life Publishers, 1977.

Morris, Van Cleve. *Philosophy and the American School.* Boston: Houghton Mifflin Co., 1961.

Murch, James DeForest. *Teach or Perish!* Grand Rapids: Wm. B. Eerdmans Publishing Co., 1961.

Nelson, C. Ellis. *Where Faith Begins.* Richmond: John Knox Press, 1967.

Newman, John Henry. *The Idea of a University.* New York: Holt, Rinehardt, and Winston, 1960.

Newman, John Henry. *The Scope and Nature of University Education.* E. P. Dutton and Co., 1958.

Niblett, W. R. *Christian Education in a Secular Society.* Oxford University Press, 1960.

North, Gary, ed. *Foundations of Christian Scholarship.* Vallecito, California: Ross House Books, 1976.

Olthius, James H. *I Pledge You My Troth.* New York: Harper and Row, 1975.

Olthius, Jean. *Teaching With Joy.* Toronto: Joy in Learning Curriculum Development and Training Centre, 1979.

Oppewald, Donald. *The Roots of the Calvinistic Day School Movement.* Grand Rapids: Calvin College Monograph Series, 1963.

Orr, James. *The Christian View of God and the World.* Grand Rapids: Wm. B. Eerdmans Publishing Co., 1954.

Painter, Franklin V. N. *Luther on Education.* St. Louis: Concordia Reprint, 1965.

Pattillo, Manning M., Jr. and Donald M. Mackenzie. *Eight Hundred Colleges Face the Future.* St. Louis: The Danforth Foundation, 1965.

Pope Pius XI. *Christian Education of Youth,* as quoted in *Selected Readings in the Philosophy of Education,* ed. Joe Park. New York: The Macmillan Co., 1958.

Priester, Marcus J. "Philosophical Foundations for Christian Education," *An Introduction to Christian Education,* ed. by Marvin J. Taylor. Nashville: Abingdon Press, 1966.

Ramm, Bernard. *The Christian College in the Twentieth Century.* Grand Rapids: Wm. B. Eerdmans Publishing Co., 1963.

Ramsay, William. "The Changing Role of the Teacher," *Dimensions in Christian Education, XVI,* No. 6 (November-December 1966): 29.

"Report of the Christian Education and Publications Committee to the Sixth General Assembly of the Presbyterian Church in America," *Commissioner's Handbook for the Sixth General Assembly of the*

Presbyterian Church in America. Calvin College, Grand Rapids: June 19-23, 1978.

Richards, Lawrence O. *A Theology of Christian Education.* Grand Rapids: Zondervan Publishing House, 1975.

_____ . *Creative Bible Teaching.* Chicago: Moody Press, 1970.

Rood, Wayne. *Understanding Christian Education.* Nashville: Abingdon Press, 1970.

Rose, Tom and Robert Metcalf. *The Coming Victory.* Memphis: Christian Studies Center, 1980.

Rushdoony, R. J. *Intellectual Schizophrenia.* Philadelphia: The Presbyterian and Reformed Publishing Co., 1961.

Rusk, Robert. *The Doctrines of the Great Educators.* New York: St. Martin's Press, 1969.

Sanner, A. Elwood and A. F. Harper, eds. *Exploring Christian Education.* Kansas City: Beacon Hill Press, 1978.

Schaeffer, Edith. *What is a Family?* Old Tappan, New Jersey, 1975.

Schaeffer, Francis A. *Back to Freedom and Dignity.* London: Hodder and Stoughton, 1973.

_____ . *The Church at the End of the 20th Century.* Downers Grove: InterVarsity Press, 1970.

_____ . "The Irrationality of Modern Thought," *Christianity Today, XV,* No. 5 (December 1970): 10-11.

_____ . *The God Who Is There.* Downers Grove: InterVarsity Press, 1968.

_____ . *How Should We Then Live?* Old Tappan, New Jersey: Fleming H. Revell Co., 1976.

Schaff, Philip. *History of the Christian Church,* Vol. II. Grand Rapids: Wm. B. Eerdmans Publishing Co., 1970.

Schenck, Lewis B. *The Presbyterian Doctrine of Children in the Covenant.* New Haven: Yale University Press, 1940.

Sherrill, Lewis J. *Presbyterian Parochial Schools 1846-1870.* New York: Arno Press, 1969.

_____ . *The Rise of Christian Education.* New York: The Macmillan Co., 1950.

Silberman, Charles E. *Crisis in the Classroom.* New York: Random House, 1970.

Sire, James W. *How to Read Slowly: A Christian Guide to Reading with the Mind.* Downers Grove: InterVarsity Press, 1978.

_____ . *The Universe Next Door: A Basic World View Catalog.* InterVarsity Press, 1976.

Skinner, B. F. *Beyond Freedom and Dignity.* Toronto: Bantam Books, 1971.

Skinner, B. F. *The Technology of Teaching.* New York: Appleton-Century-Crofts, 1968.

Skinner, Craig. *The Teaching Ministry of the Pulpit.* Grand Rapids: Baker Book House, 1973.

Smart, James. *The Teaching Ministry of the Church.* Philadelphia: The Westminster Press, 1954.

Smith, H. Shelton. *Faith and Nurture.* New York: Charles Scribner's Sons, 1941.

Spier, J. M. *An Introduction to Christian Philosophy.* Translated by David H. Freeman. Nutley, New Jersey: Craig Press, 1966.

Steensma, Geraldine J. and Harro VanBrummelen, eds. *Shaping School Curriculum: A Biblical View.* Terra Haute: Signal Publishing, 1977.

Stob, Henry J. "The Word of God and Philosophy," *The Word of God and the Reformed Faith.* Grand Rapids: Baker Book House, 1943.

Taylor, Marvin J. *Foundations for Christian Education in an Era of Change.* Nashville: Abingdon Press, 1976.

Thoburn, Robert L. *How to Establish and Operate a Successful Christian School.* Fairfax: Fairfax Christian School, 1975.

Toffler, Alvin, ed. *Learning for Tomorrow: the Role of the Future in Education.* New York: Random House, 1974.

Towns, Elmer, ed. *A History of Religious Educators.* Grand Rapids: Baker Book House, 1975.

_____. *Have the Public Schools "Had It"?* Nashville: Thomas Nelson, Inc., 1974.

Trumbull, H. Clay. *Yale Lectures on the Sunday School.* Philadelphia: John D. Wattles, 1888.

Ulich, Robert. *A History of Religious Education.* New York: New York University Press, 1968.

Vandenberg, Donald. *Being and Education: An Essay in Existential Phenomenology.* Englewood Cliffs: Prentice-Hall Inc., 1971.

Vandenberg, D. "Experimentalism in the Anesthetic Society Existential Education," *Harvard Educational Review, XXXII,* No. 2 (Spring 1962): 176.

Van Riessen, Hendrik. *The University and Its Basis.* St. Catharines, Ontario: The Association for Reformed Scientific Studies, 1962.

Van Til, Cornelius. *Essays in Christian Education.* Philadelphia: Presbyterian and Reformed Publishing Co., 1974.

Vriend, John, et al. *To Prod the Slumbering Giant.* Toronto: Wedge Publishing Co., 1973.

Warfield, B. B. *Calvin and Augustine.* Philadelphia: Presbyterian and Reformed Publishing Co., 1956.

Warshaw, Thayer S. *Religion, Education and the Supreme Court.* Nashville: Abingdon, 1979.

Waterink, Jan. *Basic Concepts in Christian Pedagogy.* Grand Rapids: Wm. B. Eerdmans Publishing Co., 1954.

_____ . *Leading Little Ones to Jesus: A Book for Mothers.* Grand Rapids: Zondervan Publishing House, 1962.

Wedderspoon, A. G., ed. *Religion Education 1944-1984.* Greenwood, South Carolina: The Attic Press, Inc., 1966.

Westerhoff, John H., III, ed. *A Colloquy on Christian Education.* Philadelphia: Pilgrim Press, 1972.

Westerhoff, John H., III. *McGuffey and His Readers.* Nashville: Abingdon, 1978.

The Westminster Confession of Faith. Richmond: The Board of Christian Education of the Presbyterian Church in the United States, 1966.

Wolterstorff, Nicholas. *Curriculum - By What Standard.* Grand Rapids: National Union of Christian Schools, 1966.

Woorell, Edward K. *Restoring God to Education.* Wheaton: Van Kampen Press, 1950.

Wyckoff, D. Campbell. *The Gospel and Christian Education.* Philadelphia: Westminster Press, 1959.

Wynn, J. C. *Christian Education for Liberation.* Nashville: Abingdon Press, 1977.

Yoder, Gideon G. *The Nurture and Evangelism of Children.* Scottdale, Pennsylvania: Herald Press, 1959.

Zuck, Roy B. and Gene A. Getz, eds. *Adult Education in the Church.* Chicago: Moody Press, 1970.

Zuck, Roy B. and Robert E. Clark. *Childhood Education in the Church.* Chicago: Moody Press, 1975.

Zuck, Roy B. *The Holy Spirit in Your Teaching.* Wheaton: Scripture Press Publications, Inc., 1963.

Zylstra, Henry. *Testament of Vision.* Grand Rapids: Wm. B. Eerdmans Publishing Co., 1958.